LECTURE NOTES

ON

PHARMACOLOGY

BY

J. H. BURN

M.D., F.R.S.

Emeritus Professor of Pharmacology, Oxford University

with a section on tropical diseases
by

L. G. GOODWIN

M.B., M.R.C.P.

TENTH EDITION

BLACKWELL SCIENTIFIC PUBLICATIONS
OXFORD AND EDINBURGH

SBN 632 08090 6

RM300
884
1971

First printed, May, 1948
Second Edition, October, 1950
Third Edition (revised), August, 1953
Fourth Edition (revised), January, 1956
Fifth Edition (revised), March, 1958
Sixth Edition (revised), August, 1961
Seventh Edition (revised), January, 1964
Eighth Edition (revised), October, 1965
Ninth Edition (revised), March, 1968
Tenth Edition (revised), January, 1971

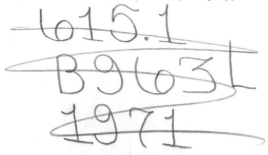

615.1
B9631
1971

Printed in Great Britain by
Alden & Mowbray Ltd
at the Alden Press, Oxford

PREFACE TO TENTH EDITION

THIS book has again been revised. There is a fuller account of polypeptides and of the prostaglandins. There is an account of dopamine and of the use of L-dopa in Parkinson's disease. The actions of etorphine and of haloperidol are described. There is an account of substances used to cause fibrinolysis. Tolbutamide and diuretics have been revised, and the action of trimethoprim is explained.

The most noteworthy revision is that by Dr. L. G. Goodwin of substances used in tropical medicine. Malaria is now important in Britain, and the discussion of medicines for other tropical diseases should prove of great value.

A student may find this book useful by looking through the index, and picking out the substances of which he knows little. He can then concentrate on them.

J. H. BURN

August, 1970

CONTENTS

LECTURE NOTES ON PHARMACOLOGY

SYMPATHOMIMETIC AMINES

Adrenaline B.P.
Epinephrine U.S.P.

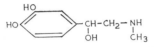

Noradrenaline B.P.
Norepinephrine U.S.P.

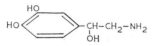

ADRENALINE and noradrenaline are amines which are found in the adrenal medulla, from which they are liberated into the blood when impulses pass down the splanchnic nerves. Noradrenaline is also accumulated in the postganglionic sympathetic nerves and their terminations. Impulses passing along these nerves release noradrenaline.

Properties of adrenaline:

1. Adrenaline increases the rate and force of the heart beat and increases the oxygen consumption of the heart. It dilates the coronary vessels. The palpitations of which people are conscious during emotion are in part due to the adrenaline released from the adrenal medulla.

2. When applied locally to blood vessels it has an intense vasoconstrictor action. When given intravenously to man as a

continuous infusion it constricts the vessels in the skin and in the intestines, but it dilates the vessels in the skeletal muscles. The sum of these effects is usually to produce little change in the blood pressure, though the heart beats faster and more powerfully.

3. Adrenaline dilates the bronchioles.

4. Arrests intestinal movement.

5. Causes a rise in blood sugar by increasing breakdown of glycogen in the liver.

6. Causes a rise of free fatty acids in the blood as a result of breakdown of neutral fat.

7. Decreases the permeability of capillaries.

8. Dilates the pupil by contracting the radial muscle of the iris.

9. Contracts the spleen.

Adenosine triphosphate (ATP) is of great importance as a source of energy. It is converted to adenosine 3', 5'-phosphate, or cyclic adenosine monophosphate (cyclic AMP) by the enzyme adenyl cyclase. Adrenaline activates this enzyme, so that the formation of cyclic AMP is accelerated. Many effects of adrenaline are due to this activation because a rise in the concentration of cyclic AMP causes many processes, such as the breakdown of glycogen to glucose, or of neutral fat to free fatty acid, to go faster.

Uses:

1. To arrest attacks of asthma. It is given by subcutaneous injection; about 0·25 ml. of the ordinary 1 in 1,000 solution is given. It can also be sprayed into the throat while the patient inhales. For this purpose a stronger solution is needed, 1 in 200. The spray must be very fine. Less palpitation is caused in this way, because less adrenaline enters the blood.

2. Adrenaline is used together with local anaesthetics when these are injected. If procaine is injected alone, its effect is brief because it is carried away from the site of injection by the blood.

If procaine is mixed with adrenaline, its effect is prolonged because adrenaline constricts the blood vessels locally and prevents the rapid removal of the procaine.

3. Adrenaline is given intravenously in anaphylactic shock to counteract the fall of blood pressure which may be fatal. It is given subcutaneously in a severe allergic attack. It can be given subcutaneously when there is great local swelling as after a sting, to diminish the capillary permeability.

4. It is injected into the heart when this has ceased to beat during an operation.

Noradrenaline (Norepinephrine)

This substance is adrenaline without the $-CH_3$ attached to the N atom. Hence this atom is 'N ohne radikal' or *nor*adrenaline.

Properties:

1. Noradrenaline differs from adrenaline in having much less inhibitor action. Thus it is very feeble as a dilator of the bronchioles and is therefore not used in asthma.

2. Because noradrenaline has less inhibitor action, it does not dilate the vessels of the skeletal muscles when it is infused intravenously in man. Consequently because it constricts the vessels of the muscles as well as those of the skin and the intestines, it causes a rise of blood pressure. This rise of blood pressure, acting through the baroreceptors in the carotid sinus and aortic arch, causes increased vagal tone and slows the heart. This reflex slowing neutralizes the direct effect of noradrenaline on the heart, which is similar to that of adrenaline, though weaker.

3. Noradrenaline has much less effect than adrenaline in causing a rise of blood sugar.

Fate of noradrenaline and adrenaline

If organs such as the heart, blood vessels, spleen, etc., which have a sympathetic innervation are extracted they are found to contain noradrenaline which is present in the sympathetic postganglionic fibres. When a slow intravenous infusion of noradrenaline is given, much of it is taken up by the sympathetic postganglionic fibres and increases the amount of extractable noradrenaline. This also happens when adrenaline is infused, but the proportion taken up is much less.

The noradrenaline and adrenaline not taken up are acted on by O-methyl transferase, so that the –OH group in the 3 position of the benzene ring becomes –OCH$_3$. The substances then formed, normetanephrine and metanephrine, are acted on by monoamine oxidase, which splits off the amine group at the end of the side chain.

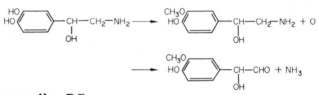

Isoprenaline B.P.

Isoproterenol U.S.P.

This substance does not occur in the body and is made in the laboratory.

Adrenaline having a –CH$_3$ group attached to the N atom has more inhibitor action on smooth muscle than noradrenaline. Isoprenaline has an isopropyl group attached to the N atom, and has still more inhibitor action than adrenaline. Thus isoprenaline is about ten times more active than adrenaline in dilating the bronchioles. It dilates all the blood vessels and so causes a fall of blood pressure. In the same way just as adrenaline accelerates the heart more than noradrenaline, so isoprenaline accelerates the heart more than adrenaline.

Use:

Isoprenaline is used to dilate the bronchioles in asthma. Route of administration:

1. By the mouth as a tablet (5 or 10 mg.) to be dissolved under the tongue. This is an inconspicuous way of treating asthma,

but as the isoprenaline is absorbed it increases the heart rate which is unpleasant for some.

2. By inhalation of a fine spray of a 1 in 200 solution. Very severe asthmatic attacks are thus relieved.

Metaraminol (Aramine)

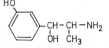

This is not a catechol amine, but is used to raise the blood pressure; it acts directly, like the catechol amines, though it is much less potent; it is much less dangerous to the heart because it does not increase the oxygen consumption of the heart. Because of the $-CH_3$ group on the carbon atom next to the amine group it is not destroyed by monoamine oxidase.

Phenylephrine (Neo-synephrine)

This is similar in structure to metaraminol, but lacks the $-CH_3$ group on the carbon; it has a side-chain like that of adrenaline. Its properties are like those of metaraminol, and it is effective in raising the blood pressure. It is used to produce mydriasis (pupil dilatation) when dropped into the conjunctival sac.

The foregoing amines act directly on the heart, blood vessels and other organs, so that if the organs lose their sympathetic nerves as a result of degeneration, the amines act not only as well as, but better than, before. Ephedrine, amphetamine and tyramine, however act indirectly.

Ephedrine B.P., U.S.P.

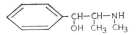

Ephedrine is also a sympathomimetic amine, but it is not a catecholamine, since it does not have –OH groups in the 3 and

4 positions of the benzene ring. Adrenaline, noradrenaline and isoprenaline are all catechol amines. Ephedrine occurs naturally in the plant *Ephedra vulgaris*. It can be taken by mouth or injected.

The rise of blood pressure caused by ephedrine is almost entirely due to the release of a small amount of the noradrenaline which is held in the postganglionic sympathetic fibres in all parts of the body. This release is not sufficient to deplete the fibres, and it is much less in amount than the release which follows the injection of reserpine. When sufficient reserpine is given all the noradrenaline in the sympathetic fibres disappears in 4 or 5 hours, and in such an animal ephedrine does not cause a rise of blood pressure.

Properties:

1. Causes a rise of blood pressure which is slower in onset and more prolonged than that caused by noradrenaline.

2. Its action on the blood pressure is increased after an infusion of noradrenaline.

3. It has some action on the brain, for if taken at night it may prevent sleep. In some persons it causes nausea and occasional dizziness.

Uses:

1. For asthma, it is taken in tablets by mouth.

2. It is used to raise the blood pressure, as in barbiturate poisoning when the cardiac output is low. It is best injected intravenously, 30 to 60 mg. Intervals between injections should be fairly long otherwise the effect of later injections diminishes.

3. It is used as a solution to be dropped into the nose in hay fever or in catarrh. A 1 per cent solution in 4 per cent glucose acts well. This constricts the capillaries of the mucous membrane.

4. It is used in combination with neostigmine in myasthenia gravis to restore the muscle strength.

Amphetamine (Benzedrine)

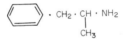

This is an amine prepared synthetically. It differs from other amines in being volatile, and it can be inhaled. It is also prepared as sulphate in tablets to be taken by mouth, 5–10 mg.

Properties:

1. It has an action on the blood pressure similar to that of ephedrine.

2. It has a stimulant action on the central nervous system, removing fatigue and causing wakefulness.

3. It diminishes appetite.

4. The dextro-rotatory compound d-amphetamine is more active on the CNS than the laevo-rotatory compound. Its approved name is dexamphetamine; Dexedrine is the sulphate.

5. When amphetamine is injected into mice the dose which is lethal for 50 per cent (LD50) depends on whether each mouse is separated from other mice or not. The LD50 for solitary mice is 100 mg./kg. but if mice are placed together in groups of ten, the LD50 is 10 mg./kg. When they are together they become very excited, and rush about in a state of panic.

Uses:

1. Is inhaled to relieve congestion of the nasal mucous membrane; it does this by causing capillary constriction.

2. Is taken by mouth because it gives a feeling of well-being and of alertness; this often results in addiction.

3. Is taken by mouth to prevent sleep; thus it is good for a motor-driver driving during the night. It enables more work to be done without a sense of fatigue. It has recently been used with success in patients with swelling of the legs, when the heart is normal, and is found to act quickly. Dose of D-amphetamine 10-20 mg. on 1-2 days. There is increased Na excretion, probably due to diminished secretion of aldosterone. Repeated use also leads to irritability and mental disturbances.

4. Is taken by mouth to reduce appetite in obesity.

Methylamphetamine (Desoxyephedrine, Methedrine)

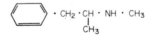

This has similar properties to amphetamine, but it is not volatile. It is said to be better than ephedrine for raising the blood pressure in man, but in animals its action is very similar. It is more powerful than amphetamine on the central nervous system, in increasing a feeling of energy and alertness and in removing sleepiness. 3 mg. methylamphetamine is equal to 5 mg. amphetamine. Its use may lead to addiction.

Tyramine

This acts indirectly by entering sympathetic postganglionic fibres and releasing noradrenaline. Its action is blocked in the presence of cocaine which prevents tyramine from entering sympathetic fibres. Tyramine is normally brief in its action on the bloodpressure, because it is destroyed by the enzyme monoamine oxidase. Inhibitors of this enzyme are often used to treat patients suffering from certain forms of mental depression. One of these inhibitors is called pargyline. In the presence of pargyline tyramine has a much longer and larger effect. Because tyramine is present in cheese, patients treated with pargyline may have a very high blood pressure when they eat cheese. Deaths have occurred. Marmite also contains tyramine.

ANTI-ADRENALINE SUBSTANCES

THESE are often called adrenergic blocking agents, but are more accurately described as anti-adrenaline substances. They are of two kinds; the one kind consists of α-blocking agents, and the other of β-blocking agents. The β-blocking agents are more important because they are clinically useful, but the α-blocking agents were discovered first.

Adrenaline causes smooth muscle to contract and it causes other smooth muscle to relax. Thus adrenaline causes contraction of the spleen, but it causes relaxation of the non-pregnant cat uterus. In causing contraction adrenaline has been said to act on α-receptors, and in causing relaxation it has been said to act on β-receptors. Both α-receptors and β-receptors may be parts of an adenyl cyclase system (see p. 2). The α-blocking agents are those which prevent adrenaline from causing contraction in smooth muscle. The β-blocking agents are those which prevent adrenaline from causing relaxation in smooth muscle. The first α-blocking agent was discovered in ergot. It is *ergotamine*. *Phentolamine* has a similar action. Patients with a high blood pressure may suffer from an adrenal medullary tumour which secretes noradrenaline and adrenaline into the blood. This can be diagnosed by injecting *phentolamine* intravenously. This causes a large fall of blood pressure within 2 minutes. See also histamine test (p. 27).

The adrenaline reversal. Both effects of adrenaline can be demonstrated in one kind of smooth muscle. Thus in a cat or a dog, an injection of adrenaline will cause a rise of blood pressure due to an increased output from the heart and also to constriction of the arteries. The constriction of the arteries is due to adrenaline combining with α-receptors and causing depolarization and contraction. When ergotamine or phentolamine is injected the α-receptors are blocked. An injection of adrenaline can then only act on β-receptors, and a fall of blood

pressure is seen. Before the injection of ergotamine or phentolamine, the action of adrenaline on β-receptors occurs, but
it is masked by the action on the α-receptors. The change in
the response to adrenaline from a rise of pressure to a fall of
pressure is called the 'adrenaline reversal'.

The relaxation of the blood vessels when adrenaline acts
on β-receptors is not a direct action. It is due to an increase in
metabolism caused by adrenaline and this increase binds calcium
to the membrane and makes it less permeable to sodium. As a
result there is hyper-polarization and therefore relaxation.

The action of adrenaline on the heart. The action of adrenaline
on the heart is not blocked by either ergotamine or phentolamine, so that when adrenaline acts on the heart it acts on
β-receptors. Its action can therefore be blocked by β-blocking
agents. The first of these was dichloroisoprenaline (or dichloroi-
soproterenol, or D.C.I.). This is not used clinically because of
its own sympathomimetic properties. A substance with a
similar side chain, propranolol (Inderal), is however used, which
is effective in blocking the action of adrenaline and of isoprenaline (isoproterenol) on the heart.

Uses of propranolol:

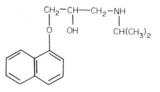

1. *Treatment of cardiac disorders of rhythm.* A simple method of
producing an arrhythmia (or disorder of rhythm) in the heart is to
infuse the glycoside ouabain into a vein of a guinea-pig at a
slow uniform rate, the guinea-pig being anaesthetized. After a
time irregularities of rhythm are seen and ventricular fibrillation
occurs causing death. If propranolol is injected first of all, these
irregularities do not occur, and there is no fibrillation. Evidently

the irregularities are triggered by the noradrenaline liberated from the sympathetic nerve endings in the heart, and if the receptors on which this noradrenaline acts are blocked by propranolol, the irregularities do not occur.

Arrhythmias are produced in the heart by some anaesthetics, notably chloroform, cyclopropane and halothane. These arrhythmias also are arrested by propranolol. Ventricular fibrillation occurring clinically has been arrested by propranolol.

2. *Angina pectoris*. This is pain over the heart which is brought on by exercise. It is due to a deficient supply of blood through the coronary vessels. Coronary disease narrows the lumen of the vessels, and lessens their ability to dilate. Whenever the heart beats faster, it requires more oxygen. When it beats faster due to exercise and cannot get sufficient oxygen because the coronary vessels dilate poorly, the heart suffers from anoxaemia, and there is pain. Propranolol stops the increase in the heart rate which is due to increased sympathetic action. When propranolol is given, a patient performs a given amount of work at a lower heart rate and he can perform a greater amount of work without feeling pain.

3. *High blood pressure*. This can be reduced by giving propranolol. The reduction of pressure is believed to be due to the block of the sympathetic impulses. Since these impulses increase the rate and force of the heart, when they are blocked the cardiac output is reduced, and therefore the blood pressure falls.

4. *Paroxysmal tachycardia*. In this condition the heart has periods in which it beats at a very high rate. The periods may last for some hours. These paroxysms are arrested by giving propranolol. This substance is more effective than any previously used remedies.

B

ACTIVE POLYPEPTIDES

1. **Oxytocin and Vasopressin.** These two substances are present in the posterior lobe of the pituitary gland. Each is a polypeptide containing 8 amino acids. In each polypeptide there is an S-S bond which can be reduced by thioglycollate. This reduction inactivates the substance.

Oxytocin causes (1) contraction of the uterus, and is particularly powerful at parturition;

(2) ejection of milk due to contraction of the myo-epithelial cells in the mammary gland.

Oxytocin is given as an intravenous drip when the action of the uterus is sluggish during childbirth and when there is no mechanical obstruction.

Vasopressin has an antidiuretic action. It is used to control the excretion of large volumes of dilute urine in the disease diabetes insipidus.

Two nuclei send fibres to the posterior lobe of the pituitary gland. One is a nucleus situated above the optic chiasma and therefore called the supraoptic nucleus. Granules from the nucleus pass along the fibres to the posterior lobe. These granules contain vasopressin attached to a carrier protein called neurophysin. Vasopressin is released from the posterior lobe after haemorrhage. It increases the permeability of the distal convoluted and collecting tubules of the kidney, so that the urine comes into equilibrium with the hypertonic interstitial fluid. In this way the antidiuretic action occurs, diminishing the water excretion.

The second nucleus is the paraventricular nucleus which forms oxytocin. This travels attached to neurophysin to the posterior lobe, from which it is released during parturition and during suckling. Oxytocin is 1000 times more active than any other substance on the rat mammary gland.

2. **Angiotensin** is a polypeptide formed by the action of the enzyme renin, which is liberated from the kidney, on a globulin

present in the plasma. The first substance formed is angiotensin I which is a decapeptide of low activity. During passage through the lungs it is converted to an octapeptide of high activity. Renin is released by stimulation of renal osmoreceptors. It does not have any role in maintaining blood pressure and the renin–angiotensin system has little relation to high blood pressure of renal origin. Angiotensin is very active in releasing catechol amines from the adrenal medulla. It stimulates ganglia. When angiotensin is injected into the adrenal artery, it causes the adrenal cortex to produce aldosterone.

3. **Substance P** is a polypeptide found in the gastro-intestinal tract, in the brain and in the retina. It is thought by some to be a transmitter of certain nerve impulses. Substance P has not been obtained pure and therefore little is known about it.

4. **Kinins.** These are polypeptides released from an inactive precursor in the plasma by an enzyme, in the same way as angiotensin is released by renin.

(*a*) Bradykinin is released by snake venom or by trypsin. The name bradykinin indicates that the substance produces a contraction of smooth muscle, but this contraction is slow.

(*b*) Kallidin is released by an enzyme kallikrein present in human saliva. Both bradykinin and kallidin cause vasodilatation.

(*c*) The sting of a wasp injects a polypeptide which greatly increases capillary permeability. Fluid passes out of the blood into the tissues causing oedema which often persists for 2 or 3 days. (A wasp sting also contains histamine and serotonin. When people die because they have been stung by a wasp, this is because of anaphylaxis; they have become sensitized by previous stings.)

The most prominent actions of kinins are those which are seen in the early stage of inflammation, namely vasodilatation, increased vascular permeability, pain and accumulation of leucocytes.

Polypeptides in disease. Polypeptides have been found present in the blood in animals suffering from disease. Thus they are present in dogs suffering from babesia and may be responsible for death. They are also present in the blood of people suffering from severe burns.

Prostaglandins. These are a family of closely related substances, the existence of which was discovered from the presence of one of them in the plasma of human semen, in which von Euler discovered a lipid which stimulated smooth muscle.

It was known that unsaturated long chain fatty acids such as linoleic acid were essential constituents of the diet. Linoleic acid is converted to arachidonic acid in the tissues and prostaglandins are synthesized from this substance. The formula of Prostaglandin A_1 is

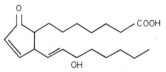

Actions. (1) When coitus has occurred prostaglandins from seminal plasma are absorbed from the vagina in amounts which affect smooth muscle tone in uterus. This mechanism may be concerned with sperm transport or with the retention of the ovum in the Fallopian tube until fertilization.

(2) Prostaglandin E_1 inhibits the release of glycerol and fatty acids from the rat epididymal fat pads, whether the release occurs normally, or whether it is in response to stimulation by adrenaline, corticotrophin, glucagon or thyroid-stimulating hormone.

(3) On the nervous system an injection of prostaglandin E_1 into the cerebral ventricles causes catatonia, in which a cat will remain for 1 to 4 hr. in any peculiar position into which it is placed. PGE_1 potentiates hexabarbitone sleeping time.

(4) PGE_1 causes a fall of blood pressure in several species. It antagonizes the vasoconstrictor action of noradrenaline, vasopressin and angiotensin.

(5) Prostaglandins are released from brain, spinal cord, spleen and the diaphragm on stimulation of the appropriate nerve, and they appear to have a close relation to chemical transmission.

THE PARASYMPATHETIC SYSTEM

THE sympathetic system is known to be active in all parts of the body during conditions of stress, as when an animal is fighting or under the influence of fear. The parasympathetic system is active in a person who is asleep after a meal. Impulses passing down the vagus nerve (1) slow the pulse, (2) quicken the movements of the intestines, (3) increase the secretions into the alimentary tract, (4) constrict the bronchioles so that breathing may be noisy. Impulses along the third nerve constrict the pupil; and diminish the amount of light entering the eye.

Parasympathetic impulses are transmitted to the end organ by acetylcholine, and the effects of acetylcholine are similar to those just described, but it has other effects as well.

Acetylcholine

$$CH_3CO \cdot O \cdot CH_2CH_2\overset{+}{N}(CH_3)_3\}Cl$$

Acetylcholine is the acetic ester of the base choline, and is commonly used as the chloride. The ester is very unstable and is readily hydrolyzed to acetic acid and choline. Acetylcholine is extremely active, while choline has very little action, about 1/1000th part of that of acetylcholine.

Properties:

1. It affects the cardio-vascular system.

Dale showed that acetylcholine acted in part like muscarine and in part like nicotine. The muscarine actions are the same as the parasympathetic actions. (Muscarine was once thought to be the substance which transmitted parasympathetic impulses. It is a highly poisonous substance present in a certain kind of toadstool called *Amanita muscaria*.)

    (*a*) A small dose of acetylcholine causes a fall of blood pressure due to vasodilatation.

(*b*) A larger dose causes vasodilatation and slows the heart in addition.

(*c*) If atropine is given, both these effects are abolished.

(*d*) A large dose of acetylcholine now causes a rise of blood pressure due to the release of adrenaline from the supra-renal gland and to stimulation of the cells of the post-ganglionic fibres of the sympathetic ganglia. The cells send impulses to the blood vessels and constrict them. This is the nicotine action, for nicotine has the same effect.

2. It increases intestinal movements and secretions.

3. It constricts the pupil and the bronchioles.

4. It causes a contraction of the skeletal muscle which is easily obtainable in the frog, and in the denervated muscle of the cat and dog. When injected into an artery leading directly into a muscle it causes contraction of the normal muscle of the cat and dog.

5. Acetylcholine stimulates the supraoptic nucleus of the hypothalamus in the same way as it stimulates sympathetic ganglia; the action on the supraoptic nucleus is exerted after giving atropine and as the fibres from the nucleus run to the posterior lobe of the pituitary gland it results in a discharge of the antidiuretic hormone.

6. Acetylcholine stimulates the receptors in the carotid body, and the impulses set up cause increased respiration.

Uses:

Acetylcholine has no uses in medicine as it is so rapidly destroyed in the body.

Carbachol (Doryl or Moryl) is a more stable ester of choline than acetylcholine. It is carbaminoyl choline. Its properties are similar to those of acetylcholine, but its action is much more prolonged.

Uses:

1. It was first used to cause contraction of the bladder in patients suffering from retention of urine in spite of absence of mechanical obstruction. The dose is very small, 0·25 mg.

2. It is used to increase intestinal movements in paralytic ileus.

Dangers:

Ampoules have been prepared for external application containing large amounts, such as 400 mg. These have unintentionally been injected, with fatal results. The correct antidote is to give atropine by intravenous injection. Death is probably due to excessive bronchiolar secretion blocking the air passages.

Methacholine is acetyl β-methyl choline. It is destroyed by cholinesterase like acetylcholine, but less quickly. It has been used to stop rapid heart rate (tachycardia) but propranolol is often much more effective.

Pilocarpine is not now much used in medicine. Its action is like that of acetylcholine, but more prolonged; it has chiefly the muscarine action, but also some nicotine action.

Use:

It is sometimes used to provoke sweating.

Arecoline has a similar action; it is used in veterinary work, especially to cause purgation in horses.

CHOLINESTERASE

Mammals possess two types of cholinesterase, which is an enzyme for hydrolysing acetylcholine. The one type is called acetylcholinesterase or true cholinesterase, and the other is called butyrylcholinesterase or pseudocholinesterase. Acetylcholinesterase is present at nerve endings where it destroys acetylcholine which has been liberated by the nerve impulse after it has fulfilled its function. It is also present in red cells. Butyrylcholinesterase is present in the glia cells of the central nervous system and in blood plasma. It may exist to destroy any overspill of acetylcholine.

Anticholinesterases

Physostigmine (eserine)

Since acetylcholine is an ester, the enzyme in the blood which destroys it is called cholinesterase. Physostigmine or eserine combines with cholinesterase and thus reduces the rate of destruction of acetylcholine. The combination does not last very long because the cholinesterase destroys the eserine and the cholinesterase is once more set free. This is an example of substrate competition; eserine competes with acetylcholine for the cholinesterase.

Uses:

1. To reduce intraocular tension when it is raised as in glaucoma. Eserine causes constriction of the pupil because it prolongs the effect of the acetylcholine liberated at the terminations of the third nerve in the sphincter iridis. It also causes contraction of the ciliary muscle which is supplied by the third nerve. This contraction narrows the ring in which the lens is suspended and thus loosens the suspensory ligament; the lens becomes more nearly spherical and the eye can then see near objects only. The constriction of the pupil causes the canal of Schlemm to open more widely and the aqueous humour drains away more easily, thus reducing intraocular pressure.

2. To increase intestinal movements when there is lack of tone as after an abdominal operation. The requisite dose must be determined with care. Excessive action is arrested by giving atropine.

Neostigmine (Prostigmin)

This is a synthetic substance with the properties of physostigmine (eserine) but its action is much more prolonged than that of eserine.

Uses:

1. Its chief use is as an antidote to d-tubocurarine when too much of this has been given to produce muscular relaxation during operations. Neostigmine restores neuromuscular trans-

mission. Doses as large as 5 mg. may be given if atropine is also given to exclude parasympathetic effects.

2. It is used in myasthenia gravis in which the production of acetylcholine at motor end-plates in skeletal muscle is below normal. One injection of neostigmine increases muscular power for about eight hours; it is given together with atropine to exclude the muscarine-like effects of acetylcholine. The effect of neostigmine is increased when it is given together with ephedrine.

3. It is used to treat retention of urine when there is no mechanical obstruction, or to treat intestinal atony.

Organophosphate anticholinesterases

Whereas physostigmine and neostigmine are carbamates, there is a group of anticholinesterases which are organic phosphates. One of these is dyflos, or di-isopropylfluorophosphonate, and another is tetraethylpyrophosphate.

Dyflos has the peculiarity that when it is injected intravenously it is not distributed throughout the body but is attached to the first tissues which it meets. When an intra-arterial injection is given to a patient with myasthenia gravis ('severe muscular weakness'), the muscles supplied by the artery, but not others, recover full power and retain it for perhaps 3 weeks. Its combination with cholinesterase is very firm and it was believed to be irreversible, but the substance pyridine 2-aldoxime will protect against dyflos. If dyflos is given daily it causes nightmares.

Edrophonium (Tensilon) is a very short-acting anticholinesterase which is used for the diagnosis of myasthenia gravis. When it is given intravenously the power of the muscles increases within a minute and the increased strength lasts about 5 minutes.

NICOTINE

THE effects produced in the body by acetylcholine after atropine has been given to paralyse the parasympathetic system, are often said to be nicotine-like effects. Nicotine is not destroyed by cholinesterase and remains attached to the receptors on which it acts; thus after an injection of nicotine the number of receptors which are free to be stimulated by another dose of nicotine is reduced, and the effect of a series of doses steadily declines until nicotine has no effect at all.

Properties:

1. Nicotine stimulates ganglia as was originally shown by Langley who applied a solution of nicotine to the superior cervical ganglion of the cat and saw that the pupil of the eye dilated. After 2 or 3 applications nicotine had no effect, and electrical stimulation of the preganglionic fibres was ineffective, although stimulation of the postganglionic fibres had its normal action. Transmission through the ganglion was blocked.

When injected into a spinal cat nicotine raises the blood pressure and accelerates the heart. This is due to

(*a*) a discharge of adrenaline from the suprarenal glands;

(*b*) stimulation of sympathetic ganglia causing (i) vaso-constrictor impulses to pass to the vessels, and (ii) cardio-accelerator impulses to pass to the heart.

Subsequent injections cause paralysis of the ganglia.

2. Nicotine stimulates the receptors in the carotid body and increases respiration.

3. Nicotine stimulates the supraoptic nucleus and liberates the antidiuretic hormone. Nicotine has several effects in the brain. If injected into the lateral ventricle it causes a fall in the general blood pressure. This fall is greater if physostigmine is injected before the nicotine. This suggests that nicotine releases acetylcholine in the brain.

If a small cup is placed on the surface of the brain, fluid collects in it from neighbouring parts of the brain and this fluid contains acetylcholine. If nicotine is injected into the lateral ventricle, the amount of acetylcholine entering the cup is increased.

Not only does nicotine increase the release of acetylcholine in the brain, but it increases the release of noradrenaline also. This can be shown by injecting labelled (or tritiated) noradrenaline into the third ventricle, and 1 hr. later perfusing artificial cerebrospinal fluid from the third ventricle to the aqueduct of Sylvius. The fluid is collected and the noradrenaline content is estimated. If nicotine (2 μg.ml.) is injected intravenously an increase in the noradrenaline is observed which may be 50 per cent.

If nicotine is injected into the ventricle of a cat which is sleeping it produces changes in the electrocorticogram indicating arousal.

Nicotine injections given intravenously in amounts equivalent per unit of body weight to the amounts present in cigarette smoke increase the rate at which rats learn to avoid an electric shock when a warning light is shown. They also double the rate at which thirsty rats will press a lever to get water.

CURARIZING SUBSTANCES

Curare is a plant extract which is prepared by certain tribes of S. American Indians. One kind of curare was kept in a bamboo-tube, and its active principle is d-tubocurarine. It is used in medicine to produce relaxation of the skeletal muscles for surgical operations. It paralyses the neuromuscular junction without affecting the function of the nerve or of the muscle.

(1) **d-Tubocurarine** causes neuromuscular block by attaching itself to many of the receptors on which acetylcholine acts. Hence the nerve impulse which liberates acetylcholine is unable to cause a muscular contraction because the acetylcholine is no longer able to depolarize the motor end-plate to a sufficient extent. d-Tubocurarine does not itself cause depolarization. Its action is antagonized by neostigmine, because this inhibits cholinesterase and therefore the concentration of acetylcholine

is raised. d-Tubocurarine causes a fall of blood pressure in some patients because it has some effect in blocking sympathetic ganglia, and because it causes a release of histamine into the blood.

Other curarizing agents are

(2) **Gallamine** (Flaxedil). This acts like d-tubocurarine, competing with acetylcholine for the receptors; it is antagonized by neostigmine.

(3) **Decamethonium** (Eulissin). The methonium compounds are substances each of which contains two quaternary N atoms. Each N has three $-CH_3$ groups as in acetylcholine, and each N is separated from the other by a chain of $-CH_2-$ groups. In decamethonium there are ten of these; in hexamethonium there are six.

Decamethonium acts like acetylcholine causing depolarization of the motor end plate and a muscle contraction. The depolarization persists, and is accompanied by a diminished excitability of the muscle itself adjacent to the motor end plate. Hence a nerve impulse can no longer cause a muscle contraction. The action of decamethonium is not antagonized by neostigmine.

(4) **Succinylcholine.** This substance can be regarded as consisting of two molecules of acetylcholine joined together. It is unstable and is therefore a safe substance to use in man because its action is transient. To obtain muscular relaxation in man it is given as an intravenous drip so that it enters the blood in a continuous stream. Succinylcholine (Scoline) is often given by the anaesthetist as a single dose when he is about to pass an endotracheal tube; he thus obtains a short-lasting relaxation.

GANGLION-BLOCKING SUBSTANCES

Just as curarizing substances interfere with the normal action of acetylcholine at the neuromuscular junction so ganglion-blocking substances interfere with the normal action of acetylcholine at ganglia, whether these are sympathetic or parasympathetic. The effect of ganglion-blocking substances is similar to that of large doses of nicotine; they cause a fall of blood pressure due to paralysis of sympathetic ganglia.

Hexamethonium. This was the first substance with this action to be used clinically for the treatment of hypertension. For this purpose it is best given by intramuscular injection, though it was often given by mouth. Since it contains two quaternary N atoms it is absorbed with difficulty from the alimentary canal and should be injected. In those with severe hypertension (eye changes such as papilloedema, intense headaches) the dose chosen is enough to compel the patient to lie down for 2–3 hours; the dose may then be effective for 8 hours in all. Hexamethonium causes postural hypotension, that is to say a fall of blood pressure which is greatest when the patient stands. The side effects are dryness of the mouth and constipation. Hexamethonium is very useful in the treatment of cardiac asthma. However it is now replaced by the following.

Pentolinium (Ansolysen) is similar in action to hexamethonium, but is more powerful.

Mecamylamine is another ganglion-blocking agent similar in action to hexamethonium, but it is not a compound containing quaternary nitrogen, and is therefore much better absorbed when given by mouth. Its action is increased when it is given together with the diuretic chlorothiazide. This diuretic makes the urine more alkaline and delays the excretion of mecamylamine. Mecamylamine being a secondary amine can get into the brain, causing tremor and other symptoms when given in large doses.

Pempidine is similar to mecamylamine, but it is more rapidly excreted. It maintains a steady hypotensive effect when given orally at 5-hourly intervals.

OTHER AGENTS USED IN TREATING HYPERTENSION

Reserpine. This is an alkaloid from *Rauwolfia serpentaria*. When injected it reduces the amount of noradrenaline present in the terminations of sympathetic postganglionic fibres in organs like the heart and blood vessels. This reduction is accompanied by a fall of blood pressure. Reserpine, however, enters the brain and has a tranquillizing action which may proceed to depression and melancholy. Reserpine must therefore be used with great care to reduce blood pressure.

Guanethidine. This is a synthetic substance which is very useful in hypertension. It is a derivative of guanidine. There is some evidence that it acts like reserpine, diminishing the amount of noradrenaline in sympathetic postganglionic fibres. There is also evidence that it blocks the effect of stimulating postganglionic sympathetic fibres so that noradrenaline is not released. As it is a very basic substance it does not enter the brain, and does not cause depression. Its chief side effect is that patients treated with it suffer from postural hypotension on getting up in the morning, and after taking exercise. Its action is prolonged. It also causes diarrhoea. Its action in blocking the release of noradrenaline, when exerted outside the body, is overcome by raising the calcium concentration of the bathing fluid.

Bethanidine has a less prolonged action than guanethidine and is useful when it is necessary to control the blood pressure quickly. The dose can be pushed up with less delay.

Chlorothiazide. This is a diuretic which increases the excretion of sodium chloride from the body. For this reason it is used also in hypertension, since the blood pressure falls when the total body sodium chloride is reduced. The loss of sodium chloride results in a fall in the plasma volume. Chlorothiazide is often used together with ganglion-blocking agents. (See p. 105.)

Alpha-methyl dopa. The pathway for the synthesis of noradrenaline begins with phenylalanine. This is converted to tyrosine, and this in turn to dopa. Thus dopa has the full name dihydroxyphenylalanine. The two –OH groups are attached to the benzene ring in the same position as in adrenaline. (See p. 1.) Dopa is then converted to dopamine by removal of the –COOH group, and dopamine is finally converted to noradrenaline by inserting an –OH group in the side chain where it is attached to the carbon atom next to the benzene ring. Alpha-methyl dopa is dopa in which a $-CH_3$ group is attached to the alpha carbon atom (i.e. the one furthest from the benzene ring, as in ephedrine, p. 5). When alpha-methyl dopa is decarboxylated, alpha-methyl dopamine is formed, and this is converted to alpha-methyl noradrenaline which is taken up by sympathetic postganglionic endings. The sympathetic impulse then releases a mixture of

Formation of adrenaline

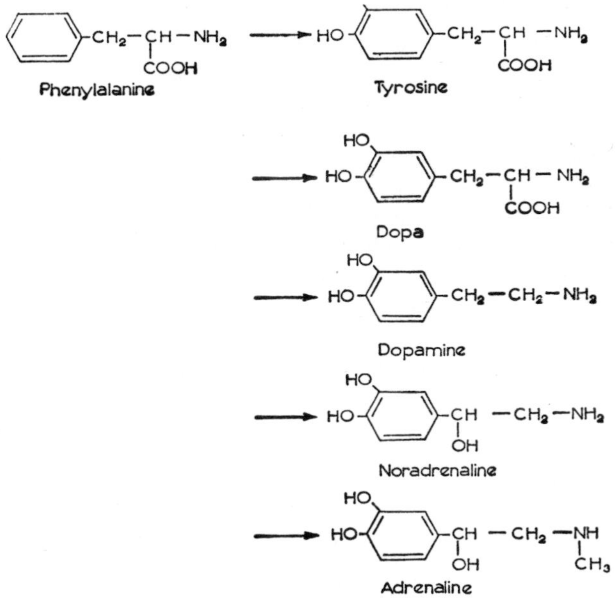

Phenylalanine

Tyrosine

Dopa

Dopamine

Noradrenaline

Adrenaline

noradrenaline and alpha-methyl noradrenaline. Since the latter substance is weaker than noradrenaline, the effect of the impulse is less than normal. Alpha-methyl dopa is therefore used in hypertension to lower the blood pressure. It does not cause postural hypotension. It is usually, but not always, effective, and it has the disadvantage that it makes some patients sleepy.

Propranolol is also used to lower blood pressure. (See p. 10.)

Dopamine has an important function in the brain. In the disease known as Parkinsonism, dopamine disappears from the corpus striatum, in which it is normally present in a concentration as high as 10 μg/g. The structure of the corpus striatum is unchanged, and the disappearance of dopamine is due to destruction of the substantia nigra in the brain stem. As a result fibres from the substantia nigra to the corpus striatum degenerate, and striatal dopamine disappears.

In Parkinsonism, patients have involuntary movements and other disabilities such as akinesia when they are unable, for example, to start walking, though when they have at last begun, they can continue. Some of these conditions are improved by giving L-dopa by mouth, which enters the brain and is there converted to dopamine. Those who have been treated with tranquillizers like chlorpromazine for a long time also develop the same motor disabilities as are seen in Parkinson's disease, and these tranquillizers are found to accelerate the turnover of dopamine into its metabolite homovanillic acid. The potency of different tranquillizers runs parallel to their effect on the metabolism of dopamine.

HISTAMINE

HISTAMINE is an amine which can be formed by removing the —COOH group from the amino-acid histidine. Histamine has the formula

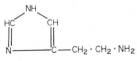

Histamine occurs in the tissues of the body and in the blood. It is destroyed in the body by an enzyme histaminase.

Properties:

1. On subcutaneous injection it causes secretion of an acid juice in the stomach; this juice contains very little pepsin.

2. It causes constriction of the bronchioles and so gives rise to dyspnoea.

3. It causes dilatation of capillaries and so leads to flushing of the skin.

4. It increases capillary permeability and so causes oedema of the subcutaneous tissues.

5. When applied locally, by pricking the skin through a drop of histamine solution, it produces the so-called triple response:

    (*a*) reddening due to capillary dilatation;

    (*b*) an urticarial weal, like a nettle sting, due to local oedema;

    (*c*) a surrounding arteriolar flare due to an axon reflex.

6. When injected intravenously histamine causes a fall of blood pressure.

Use. Adrenal medullary tumours sometimes produce a rise of blood pressure which is not a maintained rise, but is intermittent. To confirm the presence of such a tumour, histamine (0·05 mg base) is injected into the tube of an intravenous drip. A rise of pressure promptly occurs due to catecholamines released from the tumour by the histamine. Should the rise be excessive it can be reduced by phentolamine.

Importance:

Histamine is important because it is released in the body in anaphylaxis and is responsible for the symptoms of anaphylaxis.

Anaphylaxis is a condition which can occur in any animal, but it is most easily produced in a guinea-pig. If an injection of a foreign protein, such as egg albumin, is made under the skin of a guinea-pig, it becomes sensitive to egg albumin after two or three weeks, and a second injection of egg albumin then kills the guinea-pig. The death is said to be due to anaphylactic shock. In the rabbit sensitivity does not often arise in this way; for the rabbit develops antibodies known as precipitins, which circulate in its blood and neutralize the foreign protein when it is injected for the second time. The rabbit develops, not an anaphylactic condition, but an immune condition.

Anaphylaxis has been shown to be due to the formation of too few antibodies. Antibodies are produced in the cells of the tissues and usually in sufficient amount for many to leave the cells and circulate in the blood. The union of protein and precipitin in the blood has no consequences. Sometimes, however, very few antibodies are formed in the cells of the tissues so that the foreign protein enters the cells and combines with antibody there. This union, taking place inside the cell, liberates histamine.

True anaphylaxis arises in patients only in response to a foreign protein such as horse serum. Allergic phenomena arise in response to chemical substances or drugs. Workers in industry who handle certain chemicals often develop skin sensitiveness so that they suffer from capillary dilatation in the skin and from dermatitis. Those who take drugs such as quinine or aspirin sometimes become allergic and suffer from symptoms due to liberation of histamine in the body. These are dyspnoea, fall of blood pressure (sometimes making the subject unable to stand) flushing and oedema of the neck and face. The chemical substances, or the drugs, by repeated application have formed a combination with protein in the body and becoming antigenic have produced an anaphylactic state. When the symptoms are minor, the condition is said to be allergic.

Treatment:

The treatment of the acute anaphylactic or allergic condition (when sufficiently severe) is to inject adrenaline intravenously (0·25 ml. of 1–1000 solution). Otherwise the injection is given subcutaneously.

Antihistamine Drugs

Just as atropine and hyoscine are antiacetylcholine drugs, so there are antihistamine drugs. Some of the best known are:

Approved name	*Proprietary name*
mepyramine	Anthisan, Neoantergan
diphenhydramine	Benadryl
antazoline	Histostab, Antistin
promethazine	Phenergan

Properties:

1. When one of these substances is injected subcutaneously into a guinea-pig, it protects the guinea-pig against the lethal effect of histamine sprayed as a mist into a box in which the guinea-pig is placed. Histamine produces bronchospasm and death from asphyxia.

2. An antihistamine substance prevents the contraction of an isolated loop of guinea-pig ileum by histamine, and also lessens or prevents the fall of blood pressure caused by histamine.

3. Antihistamine substances prevent the triple response in the skin caused by histamine.

4. Antihistamine substances do not prevent the secretion of acid gastric juice by histamine.

Uses:

1. To remove the symptoms of hay fever.
2. To relieve urticaria, acute or chronic.
3. To lessen pruritis.
4. To reduce swellings due to insect bites.
5. For sea sickness and travel sickness.

Side effects:

1. Dryness of the mouth.
2. Mental confusion.
3. Drowsiness.

Phenergan has a prolonged antihistamine action which out-lasts the side effects. Hence it can be taken at bedtime so that the side effects pass off before morning, but the antihistamine action is still present.

There is evidence that 5-hydroxytryptamine is liberated as well as histamine in certain circumstances when antigens combine with antibodies. Symptoms such as pruritis may be due to release of 5-hydroxytryptamine. Some substances, for example cyproheptadine, are not only antihistamine but also anti-hydroxytryptamine.

Histamine-liberating Substances

Some substances liberate histamine from the tissues of the body, such as the skin and the skeletal muscles. The first substance to do this was curare, and d-tubocurarine when given intravenously causes a fall in blood pressure by liberating histamine. Stilbamidine also causes a fall of blood pressure by liberating histamine. Morphine causes pruritus (itching) in some people by the liberation of histamine in the skin. Many other substances are histamine-liberators.

Histamine in mast cells. The histamine in the skin which is released by histamine liberators is that which is present in mast cells. These cells are present in loose connective tissue often arranged in rows parallel to the blood vessels. Mast cells also contain heparin.

5-HYDROXYTRYPTAMINE
(Serotonin)

5-HYDROXYTRYPTAMINE is an amine formed by removing the –COOH group from the amino acid 5-hydroxytryptophan. This amino acid is formed from the well-known amino acid tryptophan by addition of an –OH group.

5-hydroxytryptamine is formed in cells present in the mucous membrane of the gastro-intestinal tract which are called argentaffin cells because they stain with silver. It is also formed in the brain and elsewhere in the body, and it is found present in blood platelets though it is not formed there.

p-chlorphenyalanine is a drug which inhibits the formation of 5-hydroxytryptamine in the brain. When it is given and the brain has lost its 5-hydroxytryptamine, then sleep is impossible.

The functions of 5-hydroxytryptamine are

(1) to assist in peristalsis. In the intestine peristalsis begins when the pressure inside the intestine reaches a certain threshold. This stimulates sensory nerve endings in the mucous membrane and they carry impulses to the cells of Auerbach's plexus which in turn send impulses to the intestinal muscles. 5-hydroxytryptamine sensitizes the sensory nerve endings to pressure and lowers the threshold so that peristalsis is more easily evoked. Substances like L.S.D. (lysergic acid diethylamide), which neutralize the action of 5-hydroxytryptamine, cause the threshold to rise.

(2) to assist in stopping haemorrhage. When blood clots the platelets break up and release 5-hydroxytryptamine. This has a very powerful constrictor action on small vessels.

Serotonin in the brain. Serotonin is formed from the amino acid tryptophan. When this enters the brain, it is first converted into 5-hydroxytryptophan, and this is then converted into 5-hydroxytryptamine, by removal of –COOH.

In patients suffering from depression, the administration of substances which inhibit monoamine oxidase, such as tranylcypromine, often assists in relieving the depression. Such a substance prevents the breakdown of 5–hydroxytryptamine, and this suggests that the depression may be due to a deficiency of 5–hydroxytryptamine. The beneficial effect of tranylcypromine in relieving depression has been shown to be much increased by giving tryptophan as well. This would increase the amount of 5–hydroxytryptamine, and also the amount of tryptamine itself. The benefit of giving tryptophan must therefore be due to a rise in the concentration of either one or both of these substances, which are prevented from being broken down by the tranylcypromine.

Carcinoid tumours. Tumours sometimes arise in the intestinal tract known as carcinoid tumours because they are rather like carcinomas. They are formed from cells in the intestine which stain with silver and are therefore called argentaffin. Often these tumours liberate large amounts of 5–hydroxytryptamine in the blood with the result that 5–hydroxyindoleacetic acid appears in the urine.

Patients with these tumours suffer from attacks of flushing, and it was thought that the flushing was due to the release of serotonin in the blood. But when serotonin is infused intravenously, flushing does not occur. However flushing occurs when the polypeptide bradykinin is infused. Moreover it also occurs in these patients when adrenaline is infused intravenously. Now when the salivary gland is perfused, the addition of adrenaline to the perfusing fluid causes the liberation of a kinin like bradykinin. Therefore it seemed that the flushing caused by adrenaline in a patient with a carcinoid tumour might be due to the release of a kinin from the tumour tissue. This has actually been demonstrated to occur. There is an enzyme in the tumour tissue, which forms the kinin. Possibly this kinin is substance P.

Migraine. Migraine is a condition which afflicts many people. The attack is attended by severe headache and other symptoms such as photophobia and nausea, and is characterized by pulsation in the temporal arteries. It has been thought to be produced by serotonin, and one substance which is a serotonin antagonist has been given as a prophylactic. This substance is methysergide and is 1-methyl lysergic acid butanolamide. The reports of its usefulness have varied, but on the whole have been favourable. In some patients methysergide causes dizziness and nausea and produces aching in the legs. Patients taking this substance daily have fewer and less severe headaches.

When an acute attack comes on, ergotamine is given, and this is effective.

THE BELLADONNA ALKALOIDS

PLANTS contain two types of active principle, alkaloids and glycosides. Alkaloids are organic compounds of nitrogen which act like alkalis and form salts. Glycosides are compounds containing a sugar as part of the molecule.

The Belladonna group of plants are:
   (1) Atropa belladonna, Deadly Nightshade.
   (2) Hyoscyamus niger, Henbane.
   (3) Datura stramonium.

The crude drugs are:
   (1) Belladonna Leaf.
   (2) Belladonna Root.
   (3) Hyoscyamus (dried leaves and flowering tops).
   (4) Stramonium (dried leaves and flowering tops).

The crude drugs contain the alkaloids
   l–hyoscyamine
   d–hyoscyamine
   l–hyoscine (also called scopolamine).

The two forms of hyoscyamine are separated from the leaves as a racemic mixture which is called atropine. Hence the two important active principles are **atropine** and **hyoscine.**

These two substances have different properties when they act on the central nervous system, but have similar properties when acting peripherally.

Atropine causes central excitation.

Hyoscine causes central depression.

Large doses of atropine cause a form of excitement in which the patient sees butterflies.

Both atropine and hyoscine cause paralysis of the muscarine-like actions of acetylcholine and paralyse many effects produced by parasympathetic nerves. They cause

   (1) arrest of secretions, leading to (*a*) dry mouth,
                                       (*b*) dry skin,
                                       (*c*) dry bronchioles,
                                       (*d*) dry conjunctivae;

(2) paralysis of the vagal endings in the heart;

(3) arrest of excessive contractions of the viscera.

Normal peristalsis in the intestine is not diminished, but colicky contractions are abolished. This action can be exerted in the intestines, bladder, biliary passages, and ureters. It is rarely effective in the uterus.

(4) Dilatation of the pupil of the eye and paralysis of the ciliary muscles.

Atropine is used—

(1) to produce dilatation of the pupil in iritis and irido-cyclitis when it is important to maintain dilatation for long periods. The power of accommodation for near objects is lost and only distant objects are seen.

(2) before operations to dry up the secretions of the mouth and respiratory tract which are stimulated by some anaesthetics, especially ether.

(3) to relax contractions of visceral muscle, such as the spasm of the ureter in renal colic, the spasm of the biliary passages in biliary colic and the spasm of the intestine in intestinal colic. In babies pyloric stenosis sometimes occurs and as a result the baby vomits all food; the stenosis can be relieved by giving **eumydrin** which is the quaternary form of atropine.

Hyoscine is used chiefly for its central action, which is sedative

(*a*) Together with morphine before operations.

(*b*) To quieten maniacs.

(*c*) To remove delirium tremens, a state produced in chronic alcoholism.

(*d*) In twilight sleep to produce loss of memory or amnesia.

(*e*) To prevent sea-sickness, and other forms of travel sickness. The dose is 0·5–0·6 mg. hyoscine hydrobromide.

(*f*) To remove the muscular tremors of paralysis agitans or Parkinson's disease. These are central in origin, and the action of hyoscine is probably due to blocking the action of excessive amounts of acetylcholine in the central nervous system. Tincture of Stramonium is also used in treating paralysis agitans. Other substances also used in this condition are:

benzhexol (Artane)
diethazine (Diparcol)
caramiphen (Parpanit).

Homatropine is a synthetic substance used to dilate the pupil of the eye for an ophthalmological examination. It is much shorter in action than atropine, the effect of which in the eye lasts for 2–3 days.

Methantheline (Banthine) and **propantheline** (Probanthine) are used to relieve the pain of gastric and duodenal ulcers. They are quaternary compounds and therefore are less readily absorbed from the alimentary canal and have less effect than atropine in the body generally. Since they are quaternary compounds they have a ganglion-blocking action as well as a peripheral atropine-like action. They depress the secretion of acid, but their main action in relieving ulcer pain is by lessening motility.

NITRITES

IN the group of nitrites the following substances are included:
amyl nitrite
glyceryl trinitrate
erythrityl tetranitrate.

These substances may also be classed as spasmolytics, since they relax smooth muscle. They all cause a fall of blood pressure by relaxing the smooth muscle of the arterioles.

Amyl nitrite is a volatile liquid which is obtained in small glass capsules. These are crushed in a handkerchief and the vapour is deeply inhaled. Amyl nitrite is absorbed in the lungs and the blood pressure falls within 15–30 seconds. It is used for this purpose by a person who has an attack of angina pectoris when he suffers from severe pain over the heart which radiates down the left arm. When the blood pressure falls the pain is relieved. The fall of blood pressure causes a rise in heart rate by the action of the vasomotor reflexes. The subject also appears flushed. The amyl nitrite is excreted once more through the lungs and the blood pressure soon rises again.

Glyceryl trinitrate, or nitroglycerine, is used by those who suffer from 'effort angina', which is anginal pain due to exertion. Those subject to this take glyceryl trinitrate just before they are about to exert themselves. They take it in chocolate-coated tablets which are slowly dissolved under the tongue.

Angina pectoris is believed to be the result of a temporary myocardial ischaemia caused by localized coronary artery spasm or occlusion. Glyceryl trinitrate is the drug of choice. Administration under the tongue acts within 30 seconds to 2 minutes and has a duration of action of 10 to 30 minutes. Glyceryl trinitrate or nitroglycerine causes a redistribution of coronary flow to ischaemic areas by preferential vasodilation of large coronary vessels thereby increasing collateral flow. This property is not possessed by non-nitrates such as papaverine. Other organic nitrate esters (pentaerythritol tetranitrate, erythrityl tetranitrate, mannitol hexanitrate, isosorbide dinitrate and trolnitrate) are employed in therapy because they exert their action for a longer time.

Note that amyl nitrite and glyceryl trinitrate are also useful for relieving severe pain due to biliary colic and renal colic.

Coronary Dilators

The substances of practical use for dilating the coronary vessels are the nitrites and nitrates mentioned above. Adrenaline and histamine dilate the coronary vessels but are not used for this purpose.

Thrombosis, whether in cerebral vessels or in coronary vessels occurs at sites of injury at which the platelets in the blood clump to form white masses. Clumping of platelets is increased in the presence of adenosine diphosphate, but is reduced by adenosine monophosphate. In cerebral vessels (on the surface of the brain of an anaesthetized rabbit) thrombosis has been initiated by pinching the vessels with fine forceps. An infusion of adenosine monophosphate has then removed the clumps of platelets.

THE DIGITALIS GROUP

PLANTS containing glycosides which act like the digitalis glycosides are very numerous. The best known are:

>Digitalis purpurea, the purple foxglove
>Digitalis lanata
>Strophanthus kombé
>Strophanthus gratus.

There are many different glycosides in *Digitalis purpurea* and
Digitalis lanata. The one most commonly used in this country
is digoxin, a crystalline substance obtained from *D. lanata*.
Ouabain or g-strophanthin is a crystalline glycoside from
Strophanthus gratus.

Withering in 1785 discovered the use of digitalis for treating
dropsy (oedema). He gave his patients an infusion (made by
pouring boiling water on dried digitalis leaves) which they
drank. To-day powdered digitalis leaf, biologically standardized
and compressed in tablets, is given, and also the glycosides
themselves. Thus digoxin is given by mouth, or it is given
intravenously. Ouabain is also given intravenously.

Properties of digitalis:

(1) In the normal animal, the intravenous administration of a
solution of ouabain at a uniform rate causes slowing of the
heart. This slowing is abolished by atropine and therefore the
slowing is believed to be due to increased vagal action.
There may be an increased discharge of impulses from the vagal
centre. The slowing may also be due to sensitization of the
pacemaker to vagal impulses. If the vagus is cut and stimulated,
the effect of a given stimulus is greater during the infusion of
ouabain.

(2) The second property of importance is that digitalis or
ouabain increases the force of ventricular contraction by a direct
action on the heart muscle. This can be seen in the frog heart

perfused with Ringer containing only one-third of the usual amount of calcium. If the perfusion pressure is gradually raised the output from the heart also rises up to a certain point. However any further rise of pressure does not increase the output. But if ouabain is added to the perfusing fluid, then the output rises much higher due to increased force of contraction. This action of ouabain is exerted because ouabain causes an accumulation of calcium at the site where the process of excitation of the cardiac muscle cell is coupled to contraction.

Another way of demonstrating the action of ouabain on the ventricular contraction is in the heart-lung preparation of the dog. In the presence of a barbiturate such as hexobarbitone, the force of contraction is diminished and the output is low. When ouabain is added to the blood, the force of contraction increases and the output rises.

(3) If a dog's heart in a heart-lung preparation be weakened by the injection of a barbiturate like hexobarbitone, the heart dilates and the dilatation can be recorded by enclosing the heart in a cardiometer to record its volume. The efficiency of the heart is measured as $\frac{\text{output per min.}}{\text{oxygen consumption.}}$ Since the oxygen consumption is proportional to the diastolic volume, the oxygen consumption is high and the efficiency is low when the heart is dilated. Administration of ouabain causes the heart volume to decline, so that the same work is done at a shorter length of fibre and with less oxygen consumption. The efficiency is therefore greater.

(4) It depresses conduction in the bundle of His, and may abolish it, producing heart block. This can be seen in the isolated heart.

Uses of digitalis:

(1) Digitalis is used in treating the condition known as auricular fibrillation when there is breathlessness, cyanosis and oedema due to the heart beating too quickly to act efficiently. The auricles do not contract as a single organ, but fibres or groups of fibres contract independently and the E.c.g. shows

a rate which may be 400 per minute. The ventricular rate is not as fast as this, but is very variable, and many of the beats which are felt by palpating the chest near the apex cannot be felt at the wrist. When digitalis is given:

(*a*) the ventricular rate is slowed by depression of conduction in the bundle of His so that many impulses do not reach the ventricle;

(*b*) the auricular rate is not reduced but often rises;

(*c*) the slowing of the ventricular rate is said to be in part due to stimulation of the vagus centre in the medulla, since the ventricular rate rises if atropine is given.

The benefit is thought by some to be due entirely to slowing of the ventricular rate, but it is probably also due to increased force of ventricular contraction.

(2) Digitalis is used in congestive heart failure when there is a normal rhythm, but when the heart muscle is weak. This weakness, which often occurs, for example, in the elderly after bronchitis, is shown by the presence of oedema, particularly above the ankles, and by shortness of breath. (There are many other causes besides bronchitis.) In this condition the venous pressure is too high and the cardiac output can be raised by venesection and removal of blood. The cardiac output can be raised by giving digitalis, or by giving intravenous injections of ouabain every other day until the body weight is restored to normal. The increased output of fluid in the urine may lead to a weight loss of 14 lbs. or more in the course of 3–4 weeks.

Excretion:

If the administration of digitalis or of digoxin is stopped, the ventricular rate will remain under digitalis control for 14–21 days. Thus digitalis is said to be a cumulative drug, because it is excreted very slowly.

Ouabain differs from digoxin in being much less cumulative; its effect is entirely gone after 48 hours.

Toxic effects:

Administration of digitalis in excess produces

(*a*) Bradycardia, or slow pulse. No more digitalis is given when the pulse falls to 60 per minute.

(*b*) Headache, nausea and vomiting.

(*c*) Ventricular extra systoles. The excitability of the ventricular muscle is raised, so that a normal systole is followed by an extra systole arising in the ventricle. Digitalis, digoxin and ouabain block the action of the sodium pump, and as a consequence there is a continuous loss of K^+ from the cardiac muscle cells because there is no replacement by the pump. This loss is particularly severe when chlorothiazide is used together with digitalis, and fatalities occur. Potassium chloride or acetate can be given by mouth. This neutralizes the toxic effects.

(*d*) Complete heart block.

The use of quinidine:

It was discovered by Wenckebach that patients suffering from malaria, who also had auricular fibrillation, recovered a normal cardiac rhythm when their malaria was treated with quinine. Quinine is an alkaloid from the bark of the Cinchona tree, and quinidine is another which was found to be more active than quinine on the heart.

Quinidine prolongs the effective refractory period, thus reducing the rate at which the heart can beat. Normally a second response can be produced when the intracellular potential has repolarized to only 2/3 of its full resting negativity, the rate of depolarization to the second stimulus being sufficiently rapid at this point to allow a propagated action potential to develop. Quinidine slows down the rate of depolarization, so that a subsequent response cannot occur until the membrane has had time to repolarize completely. The slowing of the depolarization phase also slows conduction. Unfortunately the normal rhythm is restored in about half the cases only. When quinidine is used the patient is first given full doses of digitalis. Quinidine is then given for 4 or 5 days. The attempt to restore a normal rhythm is not made in patients with fibrillation of long standing because in them the resumption of normal rhythm may dislodge a portion of clot which is often present in the auricular appendix.

Barbiturate poisoning. Patients who have attempted suicide by taking large doses of barbiturates, such as Nembutal, suffer from the effects of greatly reduced cardiac output. They should be given ouabain or digoxin by intravenous injection.

THE OPIUM ALKALOIDS. ANALGESICS

Opium is the dried juice obtained from the unripe capsules of *Papaver somniferum*. It contains several alkaloids of which morphine is by far the most important, constituting about 10 per cent of the opium. The only other important alkaloids are codeine and papaverine.

Morphine

Properties:

1. Is an analgesic: that is, a substance with the power to relieve pain.

2. It removes worry and anxiety.

3. It is not a hypnotic in therapeutic doses, but these doses will induce sleep when sleeplessness is due to pain. However, as the name *Papaverum somniferum* implies, large doses bring on sleep, and opium smokers go to sleep.

4. It depresses some medullary centres.

    (*a*) the respiratory centre; death from morphine poisoning is due to respiratory failure;

    (*b*) the cough centre.

5. It stimulates other medullary centres

    (*a*) the vagal centre causing a slower pulse;

    (*b*) the vomiting centre causing nausea and vomiting.

6. It stimulates the oculomotor nucleus and causes the pupil to constrict to a pin-point.

7. Small doses give rise to sweating which is accompanied by vasodilatation.

8. On the alimentary canal the first effect is that due to stimulation of the vagus centre; this leads to increased movements and to more rapid onward passage of the contents. This effect soon gives way to an action on the muscle directly, causing increased tone, especially of the sphincters. There is spasm of the ileocolic sphincter and of the pylorus; (also of the sphincter of the bladder and of the sphincter of Oddi). This leads to constipation.

9. It is a drug to which tolerance is rapidly acquired, so that more must be given to obtain the same effect.

10. It is a drug of addiction: the subject feels unhappy without it; the addict becomes untruthful and will make any promise to obtain a supply of the drug. Since he takes large amounts, his tissues become accustomed to the presence of morphine, and if the intake is stopped abruptly, the patient suffers severely. Withdrawal must be gradual; it is carried out under supervision in a home, and in the final stages the patient is narcotized with hyoscine or a barbiturate.

Uses:

1. Morphine sulphate 8–20 mg. (1/8–1/3 grain) is used before operations to allay anxiety.

2. It is used to relieve pain.

3. It is used to relieve cough, though in most cases codeine is used in preference to morphine because it does not cause addiction. Codeine is weaker than morphine, having only one-third of its power to depress the cough centre; its lesser tendency to cause addiction is probably related to its lesser power to relieve pain which is 1/20th of that of morphine. Morphine and the 4–10 times stronger diamorphine or heroin (which is the diacetyl derivative of morphine) are both used to relieve the intractable cough of a person with cancer of the lungs who is dying, or of a person with advanced phthisis, in whom the fear of addiction does not arise.

4. Morphine is used by some surgeons to treat paralytic ileus after an abdominal operation, when the intestines do not pass on their contents nor the gas inside them. This is an incorrect use of morphine since morphine causes constipation. Similarly morphine should not be used after operations on the bile passages (removal of gall stones or gall bladder) since morphine raises the intrabiliary pressure by causing spasm of the sphincter of Oddi; this results in severe discomfort.

Morphine poisoning:

The signs are: (1) slow respiration; (2) pin-point pupils; (3) cold clammy skin. *Treatment:* Give artificial respiration if necessary; wash out the stomach with 0·1 per cent potassium permanganate, as morphine even when injected may be excreted in the stomach; stimulate the respiration by intravenous nikethamide (Coramine).

Codeine is used for cough as described above.

Papaverine is a spasmolytic and is used to relax smooth muscle when this is in spasm. Papaverine is not an analgesic.

Nalorphine (N-allylnormorphine) is morphine in which an allyl group has been substituted for a methyl group attached to an N atom. This substance antagonizes the action of morphine, and is used to remove the respiratory depression caused by an overdose of morphine and to wake the patient up. When given to a person addicted to morphine it produces the painful symptoms which occur when morphine is withdrawn.

Preparations of Opium

(a) Tinctura Opii contains 1 per cent of morphine. It is used in hospital under the proprietary name Nepenthe to relieve pain.

(b) Tinctura Opii Camphorata contains 0·05 per cent morphine. It is also known as paregoric, and is used in cough medicines to relieve cough.

(c) Pulvis Cretae Aromaticus cum Opio (Aromatic Powder of Chalk with Opium). Used to check diarrhoea.

(d) Pulvis Ipecacuanhae et Opii. This is also known as Dover's Powder. It is used to produce bronchial secretion and to allay cough. The ipecacuanha contains emetine and small doses of this increase bronchial secretion. The opium allays the cough. The powder contains 10 per cent opium, 10 per cent ipecacuanha, and 80 per cent lactose.

OTHER ANALGESICS

Diamorphine or heroin is the most powerful analgesic. It is, however, a powerful drug of addiction.

Methadone (Amidone, Physeptone) is a synthetic substance equal in potency to morphine, and very similar in its properties. It is almost devoid of any constipating action in therapeutic doses.

Pethidine (meperidine, Demerol, Dolantin) has about one-fifth or one-tenth the potency of morphine, but it has two advantages:

(1) It rarely causes vomiting;

(2) It is a spasmolytic and relaxes the muscle of sphincters. It is not constipating in action. It is increasingly used during childbirth to relieve pain; it has no depressant action on the respiration of the baby as morphine has.

Phenadoxone (Heptalgin) when given by injection to man is slightly stronger than morphine. It is, however, much weaker by mouth, and its effect by mouth is unpredictable.

Aspirin is acetylsalicylic acid. It is analgesic, removing headache and much of the pain of toothache. It is also antipyretic and reduces body temperature when this is raised as in fever, but not when the temperature is normal. It reduces body temperature by increasing heat loss; there is vasodilatation and sweating. Aspirin lowers blood prothrombin and renders those with a gastric ulcer liable to haematemesis. (See sodium salicylate, p. 106.)

Phenacetin (Acetophenetidin U.S.P.). This is very similar in properties, actions and uses to aspirin. It is an aniline derivative, and has been known to cause agranulocytosis, though this is exceptional. It is present in Yeast-Vite.

Phenylbutazone has not only an analgesic and antipyretic action but it has an anti-inflammatory action somewhat like that of cortisone, and is therefore used in rheumatoid arthritis. It is also used to relieve the pain of acute gout. It is given in doses of 100 mg. four times a day, and is about six times more potent than aspirin. It has sometimes caused agranulocytosis or aplastic anaemia. Patients should be warned to report sore throat or sore mouth, fever, nausea or indigestion, because a drop in the granulocyte count may be sudden.

Etorphine is an oripavine derivative which in some species is several thousand times more potent than morphine as an analgesic. It is used together with a tranquillizing drug of the chlorpromazine group (e.g. haloperidol) to capture and transport large animals like the rhinoceros.

NARCOTICS

Including Anaesthetics
Hypnotics
Anticonvulsant substances.

Narcosis was defined by Claude Bernard as a depression of the activity of lower forms of life which disappears when the substance causing the depression is removed. Thus a narcotic is a substance which causes a reversible change. When narcotics are given to a more highly developed form of life, the condition produced is called anaesthesia and not narcosis.

ALCOHOL

(1) Action on the central nervous system.

Alcohol is still regarded by some members of the public as a stimulant, but it is classed as a narcotic because it reduces the power to do accurate work. Thus it has been shown to impair the speed and accuracy of compositors setting type, to increase the number of mistakes in typewriting, to decrease the score in rifle shooting, and to increase the time taken for a mountaineer to perform a measured climb.

The fact that many people lose their shyness and become more talkative under the influence of alcohol has then to be explained not as a stimulation of the brain, but as a disappearance of the control exercised by the highest centres which makes a person modest and self-critical.

Further evidence for the view that alcohol is a depressant and not a stimulant is that alcohol taken before going to bed acts as a hypnotic and induces sleep. This action depends on the surroundings; it is most pronounced when the subject is alone and quiet.

It is important to note that while alcohol causes increased inaccuracy in skilled work it does not incapacitate a person from doing those things he is accustomed to do. Thus a pianist may be able to continue playing a piano when he is too intoxicated to stand. In tests for drunkenness, therefore, the subject must be tested in unfamiliar ways. A drunken mechanic can still use a spanner, a drunken clerk can still write neatly.

In the Scandinavian countries and more recently in Britain the law has recognized that alcohol impairs ability to drive a motor vehicle, and the presence of more than 50 mg./100 ml. in blood is regarded as punishable in Norway. In Denmark the limit is 100 mg./100 ml. In Britain the limit is 80 mg./100 ml.

(2) Action on gastric digestion.

(a) Concentrated alcoholic solutions, especially when taken with bitters, stimulate the taste buds in the mouth and increase the psychic secretion of gastric juice.

(b) Alcohol has a direct action on the fundus of the stomach provided that the concentration is not too great; this increases the gastric secretion.

(c) Alcohol after absorption removes the feelings of worry and fatigue which depress the psychic secretion.

(d) High concentrations of alcohol, after stimulating gastric secretion at first, then inhibit it. The inhibition may last for 24 hours. High concentrations of alcohol on an empty stomach readily cause gastritis.

(3) Use of alcohol in convalescence.

(a) Since alcohol promotes a secretion of gastric juice, medicinal wines are useful in convalescence to stimulate appetite.

(b) Since alcohol is not usually allowed to athletes when in training, it must have some harmful effect on the body. It can then be argued that what is not good for an athlete is not good for a convalescent.

(4) Action on the circulation.

(a) Alcohol dilates the skin vessels, and causes a feeling of warmth. A person who has been exposed to severe cold should never be given alcohol unless he is first placed in warm surroundings. In those who take alcohol regularly the vessels on the nose often become permanently dilated.

(b) Alcohol increases the diastolic volume of the heart in

the heart-lung preparation in a concentration less than 0·1 per cent. This indicates impaired efficiency of the heart.

(5) Metabolism of alcohol.

(*a*) Alcohol is completely oxidized in the body at a rate which is unrelated to the concentration present. The rate is 10 ml. per hour (reckoned as absolute alcohol). The relative harmlessness of ethyl alcohol is due to this rapid oxidation. Methyl alcohol is much more toxic than ethyl alcohol because it is oxidized very slowly, formic acid being formed; it produces coma which may last for some days, and inflammation of the optic nerve and retina which may end in blindness.

(*b*) Alcohol is a food, since the energy of oxidation is available to the body. Glucose is, however, equally useful and also rapidly absorbed.

Alcohol poisoning:

Keep warm; apply artificial respiration if necessary; wash out the stomach. Intravenous injection of insulin and glucose (10 units insulin, 20 g. dextrose in 400 ml. by drip) is recommended.

Alcohol addiction:

This can be cured by giving **disulfiram** (Antabuse) which is a substance able to arrest the oxidation of alcohol at the stage of acetaldehyde. The accumulation of acetaldehyde makes the subject feel wretched and ill. Disulfiram should be used only under medical supervision.

ANAESTHETICS

Alcohol is similar in some respects to the two volatile anaesthetics chloroform and ether, and mixtures of all three used to be used.

Ether. The advantages of ether are:

(*a*) that it is completely efficient and very safe in use. Many anaesthetics produce unconsciousness, so that the subject cannot feel; this is, however, not enough, for the surgeon cannot operate unless there is muscular relaxation as well. There must be not only anaesthesia but also a disappearance of the reflexes which cause muscular contraction in response to sensory impulses. Ether is highly efficient because with its aid full muscular relaxation is easily possible. Some anaesthetics are dangerous because when given in sufficient amount to cause muscular relaxation they may also paralyse the respiration. Ether is very safe because there is a wide margin between the amount required to cause 'surgical anaesthesia' and that required to paralyse respiration.

(b) Ether is administered through the lungs and is exhaled in the expired air. If the depth of anaesthesia threatens to arrest respiration, the anaesthesia can be lightened immediately by giving less. Ether can thus be administered by unskilled persons.

The disadvantages of ether are:

(a) that it is irritant to the respiratory passages; during induction of anaesthesia the irritation may cause laryngeal spasm so that the subject will not breathe. The irritation also results in the secretion of much mucus. This is always minimized by giving atropine beforehand, but it is impossible to know the correct dose for each patient so that atropine is only partially successful. Some of the smaller bronchioles are blocked with mucus and remain so after the operation is over; the alveoli where this occurs do not expand during respiration and bronchopneumonia arises. The risk of post-operative pneumonia is diminished by making the patient take deep breaths, or by giving him air containing 5 per cent CO_2 to breathe from a bag. This should be done several times during the two days after the operation.

(b) Ether causes much post-operative vomiting, which is extremely distressing to the patient.

(c) The patient takes several days to recover from the effects of ether; this may be due in part to the weakening of the heart caused by ether, which although not so serious as that caused by chloroform is still considerable. This action of ether was demonstrated by Dale in the following way. He injected histamine into a normal cat and showed that it was unaffected by a large dose. He gave the cat ether as an anaesthetic but made no operation. After the cat recovered from the ether, it was then found to be severely affected by a dose of histamine one-tenth the amount it received previously. The same difference was caused by chloroform, but nitrous oxide had no action of this kind.

(*d*) Induction of anaesthesia with ether is slow owing to the high concentration necessary in the blood.

(*e*) Ether is inflammable.

Chloroform. The advantages are:

(*a*) That it is more potent than ether, since 2 per cent of chloroform will maintain anaesthesia as well as 8 per cent ether. A smaller bulk will therefore maintain anaesthesia for the same time.

(*b*) It is not so irritant as ether, so that induction with chloroform is smoother and the patient resists less.

(*c*) It is not explosive.

The disadvantages of chloroform are:

(*a*) That sudden death due to ventricular fibrillation may occur during induction. This may be related to the observation that ventricular fibrillation can be produced in dogs anaesthetized with chloroform by injecting adrenaline.

(*b*) That it causes excessive vagal slowing; but this is prevented by giving atropine beforehand.

(*c*) That it may lead to delayed chloroform poisoning in which there is persistent vomiting, jaundice and fatty degeneration of the liver and kidneys. It occurs about 24 hours after the anaesthetic. Animals given a high protein diet beforehand are much more resistant to this toxic action of chloroform on the liver.

Other substances produce the same effect, namely carbon tetrachloride and similar chemical substances such as are used in dry cleaning.

(*d*) Chloroform greatly weakens the heart.

These disadvantages have almost eliminated chloroform from use.

Nitrous oxide. The advantages of nitrous oxide are:

(*a*) That it is an anaesthetic from the effects of which recovery is almost always immediate and complete. It is therefore useful for operations after which the patient shortly returns home.

(*b*) It does not produce circulatory changes or post-operative vomiting; it is not irritant.

The disadvantages of nitrous oxide are:

(*a*) That only very high concentrations in the inspired mixture, from 89–94 per cent, produce complete loss of feeling. This leaves room for only 11–6 per cent of oxygen, so that there is some cyanosis.

(*b*) That nitrous oxide is unable to produce muscular relaxation unless a pressure chamber is used, and this for practical purposes is impossible.

Uses of nitrous oxide are:

1. For tooth extractions when the pure gas is breathed until the patient is deeply cyanosed. A period of 30–45 seconds is then available for the extraction.

2. Together with oxygen after a basal anaesthetic has first been given to produce partial anaesthesia.

Ethyl chloride

This is a powerful anaesthetic resembling chloroform which is used only for the induction of anaesthesia and for short operations on children. Induction is specially rapid, and when complete the anaesthetic is changed, e.g. to ether, which is much less toxic.

Cyclopropane. The advantages of cyclopropane are:

(*a*) that like nitrous oxide it is remarkably free from after effects such as post-operative vomiting and shock, so that the patient's condition is not adversely affected by it.

(b) It is not irritant.

The disadvantages of cyclopropane are:

(a) That although muscular relaxation can be obtained with cyclopropane, the margin between the concentration (which may be 20–45 per cent) required to cause relaxation and the concentration which stops the respiration is small. Cyclopropane can only be given by an expert.

(b) That it is expensive and must therefore be given in a closed circuit apparatus.

(c) That it is explosive.

Halothane (Fluothane) is a liquid which is derived from ethane and contains fluorine. It is not explosive and does not burn. It is a powerful anaesthetic, free from irritant properties, but it weakens the heart like chloroform and it causes a fall of blood pressure. It does not affect the liver like chloroform. It readily produces muscular relaxation, and anaesthetists like it for operations in which a muscle relaxant has been given. If the effect of the relaxant is wearing off, muscular relaxation can be maintained by giving more halothane. It causes anaesthesia when no more than 1·5 per cent is present in the mixture which is being breathed. It is essential to administer halothane in a concentration which is precisely known.

ANAESTHETICS GIVEN BY INJECTION

The most common anaesthetics for use by injection are barbiturates, which is the common name for derivatives of barbituric acid.

Barbituric acid is formed by the condensation of malonic acid with urea

$$\begin{matrix} H \\ \diagdown \\ C \\ \diagup \\ H \end{matrix}\begin{matrix} COOH \\ \\ \\ \\ COOH \end{matrix} + \begin{matrix} NH_2 \\ \diagup \\ CO \\ \diagdown \\ NH_2 \end{matrix} = \begin{matrix} H \\ \diagdown \\ C \\ \diagup \\ H \end{matrix}\begin{matrix} CO—NH \\ \diagup \diagdown \\ \quad CO \\ \diagdown \diagup \\ CO—NH \end{matrix} + 2H_2O$$

Barbituric acid itself is not a narcotic, but when the hydrogen atoms attached to the carbon atom are substituted, many compounds so formed are narcotics. Barbiturates are used for three purposes:

(1) As complete anaesthetics.
(2) As hypnotics (to procure sleep).
(3) In the treatment of epilepsy as anticonvulsants.

As anaesthetics **thiopentone** (thiopental, Pentothal) and **hexobarbitone** (Evipan) are used. When injected intravenously they produce anaesthesia and muscular relaxation within a few seconds. They must be injected slowly since otherwise they paralyse the respiratory centre and it is common to ask the patient to count in order to follow the effect of the anaesthetic on him. There is no stage of excitation, and the passage into unconsciousness occurs without warning, so that the anaesthetic is ideal for the patient's comfort.

Both thiopentone and hexobarbitone have a short action because they are absorbed from the blood into the fat depots. If a longer period of anaesthesia is required, more may be given. On account of the danger of respiratory failure these anaesthetics should only be used by those who know how to deal with respiratory arrest.

Some anaesthetists give thiopentone together with tubocurarine; they should not, however, be given simultaneously because of the great variation in the response of different individuals to both thiopentone and tubocurarine. It is for this reason impossible to know beforehand what is a safe initial dose.

HYPNOTICS

Chloral is the oldest synthetic hypnotic. It is trichloracetaldehyde; it is ordinarily used as a hydrate, the formula of which is $CCl_3 \cdot CH(OH)_2$. It is very similar in composition to bromethol except that it contains Cl and not Br. The dose to send a patient to sleep is 5–20 grains (0·3–1·3 g.). In the stomach it has an irritant action and may cause vomiting. To prevent this, it should be given well diluted. In the body it is first reduced to an alcohol, and then combined with glycuronic acid, to be excreted in the urine as urochloralic acid. It is much used in midwifery.

Bromethol (Avertin) is tribromethyl alcohol. It is administered per rectum dissolved in amylene hydrate. It is used in toxaemia of pregnancy. It is conjugated in the liver with glycuronic acid and is excreted in the urine as urobromic acid.

Paraldehyde is a volatile liquid soluble in 10 parts of water. It is rapidly absorbed when given by mouth or by the rectum, and it is excreted unchanged in the breath and in the urine. It has no depressant action on the heart as chloral has (chloral is a relative of chloroform), and it is considered a very safe hypnotic, though on account of its unpleasant smell the patient's breath is affected. For this reason it rarely causes addiction.

Paraldehyde can also be given by intramuscular injection to restless or noisy patients who will not stay in bed. It acts with great rapidity. Dose 8 ml.

Barbiturates as hypnotics:

Barbiturates are used as hypnotics in different ways.

(1) Tablets of **sodium hexobarbitone** are used for persons who sleep quite well once they have fallen asleep, but who cannot get off to sleep. Such tablets were used for Air Force pilots during the war, who were living under considerable strain. The effect of hexobarbitone has completely gone in 1-2 hours.

(2) Tablets of **butobarbitone** (Soneryl) are used to ensure a good night's sleep either for a patient in hospital or for a normal person travelling by night train. He wakes fresh in the morning.

(3) Tablets of **barbitone** (Veronal) or **barbitone sodium** (soluble barbitone, Medinal) are often used for chronic sleeplessness, but both are apt to accumulate in the body, since only half is excreted in the first 24 hours, and they can be detected in the urine for 14 days. If it is taken regularly barbitone produces forgetfulness, and it is said that patients have taken a second dose because they have forgotten taking the first dose. After an overdose patients pass into a profound sleep from which they cannot be aroused. Breathing becomes shallower.

Barbiturate poisoning. Many attempts are made to commit suicide by taking barbiturates. Barbiturates depress the heart and diminish the cardiac output, and they cause a fall of blood pressure. Patients often develop bronchopneumonia because of the poor circulation. The circulation can be much improved by injecting ouabain (or strophanthin) intravenously to increase cardiac output. It can also be improved by intravenous injection of ephedrine (30 mg) repeated every hour. Stimulants like megimide are useless.

(4) In mental hospitals where it is desired to keep patients asleep for long periods while under observation, **phenobarbitone** (Luminal) is given. This is still longer in action than barbitone.

Sulphonal is a cumulative hypnotic (not a barbiturate) which is dangerous. It is used under supervision in asylums when other drugs have failed to quieten maniacs. It gives rise to the appearance of porphyrin in the urine, which turns red.

Before leaving hypnotics it is worth mentioning
Sedormid,
Carbromal (also called Adalin).

These are derivatives of acetylurea. Both are mild and are broken down in the body. They can be used when it is desired to avoid a barbiturate. Sedormid has been found to cause purpura.

ANTICONVULSANTS

This term has been applied to substances used in the treatment of epilepsy, in the course of which patients suffer from convulsions. **Sodium bromide** is the oldest remedy. Potassium bromide and ammonium bromide have the same action. When taken by mouth sodium bromide is absorbed as is sodium chloride; sodium bromide has a specific depressant action on the motor cortex. It is usually given in a dose of 1 g. three times a day.

Epileptics who regularly take bromide develop bromism. This is a condition in which the patient has a pustular rash on his face, and in which he has become dull and stupid; he salivates freely. The rash is probably due to the excretion of bromide by the skin just as chloride is excreted, and the bromide passing through the sweat glands causes the pustules to appear. Bromism is treated by giving additional chloride in the diet, for this increases the excretion of chloride by the kidney. The amount of bromide excreted by the kidney is in direct proportion to the amount of chloride excreted.

Conversely when it is desired to obtain the maximum effect with the minimum dose of bromide, the chloride in the diet is reduced. Normally the daily intake is 10 g. sodium chloride. It is easy to reduce this to 3 g., and with more trouble to 1·5 g.

Sodium bromide is also used as a hypnotic to enable nervous subjects to get to sleep. Since it tastes like salt, it can be given in a cup of Oxo or Bovril.

Phenytoin is the safest remedy for the various forms of epilepsy, though it is not a barbiturate but is a diphenyl-hydantoin. It was discovered in a laboratory search for substances which would depress the excitability of the motor cortex to electrical stimuli applied outside the skull of cats. One disc-shaped electrode was applied to the top of the cat's head and the second was put inside its mouth. The minimal stimulus which would evoke convulsions was determined before and after giving the substance being tested.

Primidone (Mysoline) is the most effective agent for the form of epilepsy known as 'grand mal'. It is less toxic than other drugs, and does not make the patient sleepy. This is an advantage over **phenobarbitone,** which has long been used for 'grand mal'.

Phenobarbitone is usually given three times a day in a dose of 30 or 60 mg. ($\frac{1}{2}$ or 1 grain) and care should be taken to space the doses evenly over the 24 hours. The form of epilepsy known as 'petit mal' is sometimes made worse by phenobarbitone. For such patients **troxidone** (Tridione) is used, but it is very toxic.

Phemitone (Prominal) is methylphenobarbitone. It is better than phenobarbitone for reducing the number of epileptic fits.

TRANQUILLIZING DRUGS

THESE are substances which produce calmness and which remove anxiety without affecting mental clarity. There are two kinds. The one is used in psychosis where the mind is deranged, especially in schizophrenia. The other is used in neurosis where the mental disturbance is functional, and in normal people under emotional strain.

Drugs used in psychoses. Reserpine has the property of producing tranquillity. In the hypothalamus and in the tegmentum of the midbrain noradrenaline is present, and in parts of the limbic system serotonin is present. When reserpine, or a related substance having the same property, is given, the noradrenaline and the serotonin diminish in amount. If enough is given they may disappear. How this disappearance of these amines leads to tranquillity is not known. Reserpine also has an action in the peripheral nervous system, where it causes noradrenaline to disappear from sympathetic postganglionic fibres, and this leads to a failure of sympathetic activity. But in the brain the disappearance of noradrenaline does not impair the nervous discharge recorded in the preganglionic fibres of the sympathetic system in the cat.

The difficulty in using reserpine as a tranquillizer is that its effect may go beyond the production of tranquillity and lead to depression and melancholy. Suicides have occurred.

Chlorpromazine and related substances are therefore the principal substances now used. These are all derivatives of phenothiazine.

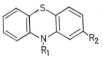

In chlorpromazine R_1 is $= CH_2.CH_2.CH_2.N(CH_3)_2$ and R_2 is Cl. When chlorpromazine is given, the electroencephalogram shows changes in the formatio reticularis; in the region responsible for wakefulness and arousal, the threshold to stimuli such as pain, electric currents and adrenaline is raised, and the responses are short. However, the therapeutic effects of chlorpromazine may be due to changes in the limbic system, where high doses cause bursts of spikes which originate in the amygdala.

It is possible that the therapeutic effect is due to inhibition of powerful drives kept up by pathological processes in the brain, and chlorpromazine may inhibit the metabolic processes in these areas.

Chlorpromazine inhibits many enzyme reactions; it has a powerful effect in reducing body temperature, and has an anti-emetic action. The side effects which are met in clinical practice include dry mouth, low blood pressure and constipation. There is engorgement of the breasts and a flow of milk. High doses produce symptoms of Parkinsonism, spasticity and tremor. The amount of dopamine in the caudate nucleus is not diminished, but its turnover is increased as shown by an increase in the amount of its metabolic product homovanillic acid.

There are, in addition, severe toxic effects, jaundice, skin rashes and depression of the bone marrow.

Some of the compounds allied to chlorpromazine are trifluoperazine (Stelazine), thioridazine (Melleril) and perphenazine (Fentazine).

Haloperidol is the prototype of a new group of drugs which was developed from a study of the actions of substances related to pethidine. These drugs are tranquillizers which act like *chlorpromazine* but in amounts 100 to 500 times smaller. A particularly active analogue is *spiperone* and this is used in operations on animals like sheep and goats. The trauma and disturbances of full anaesthesia are avoided, yet there is no sign that the animal is disturbed or frightened. It is not necessary to restrain it. Restless and non-cooperative sheep can be quietened by a small dose so that they remain indifferent to manipulations for 3 hours, and they feed during the period. Such a drug removes fear without affecting conciousness.

These tranquillizers produce their effect in the absence of any action on noradrenaline, 5-hydroxytryptamine or acetylcholine. But their tranquillizing potency runs parallel to their effect on the metabolism of dopamine. Thus the same effect on the metabolism of dopamine was obtained by 10 mg./kg. chlorpromazine as by 0·1 mg./kg. spiperone which have similar tranquillizing effects.

Uses:

For relief of restlessness and agitation, especially in old age. For acute and chronic schizophrenia in the control of disturbed behaviour. In the management of patients in senile dementia who have disturbed behaviour and who are living at home.

Drugs used in neuroses. **Methylpentynol** (Oblivon) reduces apprehension in those about to visit the dentist, and has been used for the same purpose by those about to commit a crime.

Other substances are benactyzine, hydroxyzine and meprobamate; they vary in their properties.

Meprobamate when given to monkeys and rats makes them manageable and fearless, but the loss of fear does not lead to loss of conditioned reflexes. Thus rats learn to avoid an electric shock when this is preceded by ringing a bell. Under the influence of meprobamate the rats still avoid the shock, but under the influence of benactyzine or of hydroxyzine they do not. Although meprobamate has properties of unusual interest from the pharmacological point of view, some physicians consider that it has only limited uses as compared with the much cheaper barbiturates.

Action and Uses:

These substances do not have the profound effects on brain metabolism which are exerted by reserpine and by the phenothiazine drugs, and nothing is known about the biochemical side of their action. Proof of the efficiency of benactyzine in man is still lacking. Hydroxyzine appears to relieve anxiety without impairing critical faculties. Meprobamate has been shown to improve patients with anxiety neuroses and even with certain psychoses. In contrast to other tranquillizers it did not impair performance in psychological experiments involving concentrated effort, so that meprobamate is capable of checking emotional responses while not interfering with skill and rational behaviour.

LOCAL ANAESTHETICS

LOCAL anaesthetics are substances applied locally to paralyse sensory nerve endings. The first substance recognized to possess this property was cocaine, which is present in Coca leaves. These leaves were chewed by South American natives working in the silver mines of the Andes, and under the influence of the cocaine present in the leaves they were able to perform work for longer periods than otherwise. This property of cocaine is unrelated to its local anaesthetic action.

Cocaine hydrochloride is a local anaesthetic which must be used cautiously since it is not free from danger. It should not be given by injection because of the danger of cardiac or sometimes respiratory arrest and should be reserved for superficial application:

(1) To the eye. It is absorbed through the conjunctival mucous membrane and produces in the eye

(*a*) local anaesthesia.

(*b*) pallor; this occurs because cocaine constricts the blood vessels by increasing the effect of adrenaline in the blood. It increases the effect of adrenaline and of noradrenaline by blocking the uptake of these catecholamines by the sympathetic postganglionic fibres.

(*c*) dilatation of the pupil; this occurs because cocaine stimulates the radial muscle of the iris for the same reason as it constricts blood vessels.

(*d*) widening of the palpebral fissure, due to increased contraction of Muller's muscle.

(2) To the mucous membrane of the nose and throat. Cocaine solution is commonly applied by a spray or on a swab of cotton wool. The total amount applied should not exceed 0·1 g.

Other properties of cocaine:

1. Cocaine produces central excitement and is a drug of addiction. Unlike morphine, cocaine does not lead the addict

to seek solitude. Cocaine is commonly taken like snuff and absorbed from the nasal mucous membrane.

2. The power of cocaine to diminish physical fatigue is probably due to its power to prolong the action of adrenaline and noradrenaline which increase the force of muscle contraction in fatigue. This action of cocaine is due to inhibition of the uptake of noradrenaline and adrenaline by sympathetic fibres, so that the concentration of these amines in the blood rises.

3. Toxic doses of cocaine lead to restlessness and finally convulsions. The respiration becomes very irregular and may fail suddenly. The risk of toxic symptoms arising is diminished by giving the patient a barbiturate beforehand (such as phenobarbitone or Luminal 1 grain).

Procaine (Novocain) is a synthetic substance, a derivative of aniline,

$$NH_2 \left\langle \bigcirc \right\rangle CO \cdot O \cdot CH_2CH_2N(C_2H_5)_2$$

which is less potent and much less toxic than cocaine. It does not readily pass through mucous membranes and therefore cannot be applied superficially like cocaine. It is used for injection under the skin or into the gum, when it is mixed with adrenaline to constrict the vessels and so prevent its dispersal by the blood stream. Thus it is absorbed slowly into the circulation and the liver destroys it as it enters. As much as 30 ml. of a 0·5 per cent solution of procaine combined with adrenaline can be given without producing any effect on the brain. It is also employed for conduction anaesthesia of nerve trunks.

Cinchocaine (Nupercaine, Percaine) is a synthetic local anaesthetic stronger even than cocaine and not proportionally more toxic. Hence if care is taken to see that the proper concentration is used, it is safe in use. Cinchocaine, tested intradermally in guinea-pigs, is three times stronger than cocaine, while cocaine is seven times stronger than procaine. Thus cinchocaine is about twenty times stronger than procaine. Procaine is injected under the skin in solutions from 0·5 to 2.0 per cent, while cinchocaine is used from 0·01 to 0·05 per cent, adrenaline being mixed with both. Cinchocaine is also used for spinal anaesthesia.

Lignocaine (Lidocaine, Xylocaine) is a useful anaesthetic for producing nerve block and for infiltration anaesthesia. It is also used for spinal and for surface anaesthesia. It is used in $\frac{1}{2}$–2 per cent solution with adrenaline; it acts rapidly.

Amethocaine (tetracaine, Decicain) is a powerful local anaesthetic used for spinal anaesthesia. Amethocaine can be applied to the mucous membrane like cocaine or it can be injected.

Butacaine (Butyn) is too toxic for injection but is widely used as a surface anaesthetic for the eye and nose, and in ointments.

Phenacaine (holocaine) is prompt in action and is used especially for the eye.

Benzocaine (ethyl aminobenzoate), **butyl aminobenzoate** and **orthocaine** (Orthoform) are sparingly soluble, and when applied in ointments and powders produce a prolonged anaesthetic effect without the absorption of toxic amounts.

SUBSTANCES WHICH STIMULATE THE BRAIN

Inhibitors of monoamine oxidase. Amines such as serotonin (5–hydroxytryptamine), tryptamine, tyramine and dopamine are destroyed by the enzyme monoamine oxidase, which removes the amine group in the form of ammonia. The effect of these amines is therefore prolonged when this enzyme is inhibited.

Various substances have been found to inhibit this enzyme, and these substances are useful in psychiatry to relieve endogenous depression. One of the first substances used for this purpose was iproniazid (Marsilid), but tranylcypromine (Parnate), phenelzine, pargyline, nialamide and others are now more commonly used. When these inhibitors are given there is very often an elevation of mood and disappearance of depression. The beneficial effect of these drugs suggests that one or more of the amines mentioned above is deficient in endogenous depression, and that the depression is due to this deficiency. It is known that serotonin and dopamine are present in the brain, and endogenous depression may be caused by a deficiency of one of these.

There is evidence which suggests that serotonin may be the responsible amine. Thus it has been found that when tranylcypromine was given, not alone, but together with tryptophan, then the improvement in patients was very much greater. Tryptophan may follow one of two pathways. It may be first converted into 5–hydroxytryptophan, and then converted by removal of –COOH into serotonin. Or tryptophan may be directly converted by removal of –COOH into tryptamine. If the first pathway is followed, then the giving of tranylcypromine will prolong the period of action of the serotonin. If the second pathway is followed, tranylcypromine will prolong the period of action of tryptamine.

The other amine present in the brain which is destroyed by monoamine oxidase is dihydroxyphenylethylamine, or dopamine. Attempts have been made to see if the giving of dopa together with the inhibitor pargyline would have a beneficial effect in states of depression, but no evidence that this combination has a beneficial effect has been obtained.

Effect of beans. The pods of broad beans contain dopa, so that when such beans are eaten together with the pods, dopa is ingested. This is converted to dopamine and destroyed in the body by monoamine oxidase, which is present in the peripheral tissues such as the liver as well as in the brain. In patients taking inhibitors of monoamine oxidase, the dopamine is not destroyed, and causes a large rise of blood pressure.

Cheese. Many kinds of cheese contain tyramine which is the amine formed by removal of –COOH from tyrosine. The amount of tyramine in cheese is very variable, and has been found as high as 1·5 mg. per g. Tyramine is normally destroyed by monoamine oxidase, but patients taking an inhibitor do not destroy it, and severe clinical effects consequent on the rise of blood pressure have followed; three cases of intracranial haemorrhage have been described.

Yeast extracts like Marmite contain tyramine and may have a similar effect on those taking a monoamine oxidase inhibitor.

Imipramine and amitriptyline. These substances are also used in treating endogenous depression but they do not inhibit the enzyme monoamine oxidase. They have a similar action to that of cocaine. When noradrenaline is released from a sympathetic nerve ending, some of it acts on the receptors to produce a physiological effect, and some of it is taken up again into the sympathetic fibre. Cocaine blocks the uptake into the fibre, and therefore the amount of noradrenaline acting on the receptors is increased. Imipramine and amitriptyline have the same action. Cocaine causes stimulation in the brain, and this stimulation may possibly be due to an action like that at the sympathetic nerve ending, so that there is a rise in the concentration of free noradrenaline. If this is so, imipramine and amitriptyline may act in the same way.

Caffeine is a derivative of xanthine which is nearly related to uric acid. Caffeine is trimethylxanthine. A cup of tea or coffee contains an amount of the order of 1 mg. per ml. Very little of the caffeine which enters the body forms uric acid.

Properties:

1. It increases the calculating power of the brain; the speed of mental arithmetic is greater. In excess it causes sleeplessness.

2. It decreases fatigue, and increases the amount of muscular work which can be done.

3. It is a medullary stimulant, stimulating the respiratory centre in particular.

4. It increases the rate of the heart by a direct action on the heart, and causes coronary dilatation.

5. It relaxes smooth muscle.

6. It acts as a diuretic, causing an increased flow of urine by diminishing the amount of fluid absorbed by the tubules. It has been shown to increase the number of active glomeruli in the frog, and it also dilates the afferent vessels to the glomeruli; both these actions have been thought to contribute to the diuretic action.

Theophylline is dimethylxanthine. Asthmatics sometimes become so ill that adrenaline is ineffective in relieving their bronchial spasm. The intravenous injection of theophylline may then save the patient's life. Theophylline is not very soluble in water and is prepared in solution in ethanolamine or other solvents such as ethylene diamine.

Light has recently been thrown on the action of theophylline.

Various substances, or hormones, such as adrenaline, ACTH, vasopressin, insulin, glucagon (and several others) have been shown to increase the intracellular concentration of cyclic AMP, and the action of these substances is due to this increase. Cyclic AMP is broken down by phosphodiesterase to the inactive 5-AMP, but this breakdown does not occur in the presence of theophylline. Thus theophylline increases the concentration of cyclic AMP. See p. 2.

This explains the action of theophylline in relieving the bronchial spasm of status asthmaticus. Theophylline intensifies the action of the noradrenaline released at the sympathetic terminals in the bronchioles. The noradrenaline acts by activating adenyl cyclase which converts ATP to cyclic AMP. The cyclic AMP is responsible for the bronchial dilatation. Theophylline prevents the cyclic AMP from being broken down.

Propranolol prevents adrenaline or noradrenaline from activating adenyl cyclase.

Leptazol (also called Metrazol or Cardiazol) is used to produce convulsions in patients with schizophrenia; it stimulates the motor cortex. This treatment began for theoretical reasons, but it has been shown in rats that it restores conditioned reflexes which have faded through lack of reinforcement.

Nikethamide (also known as Coramine) is an excellent respiratory stimulant when the respiration is depressed by morphine. It is a harmless substance even in large doses, and is often used in hospital in the hope that it will restore the blood pressure and strengthen the heart. It is difficult, however, to find any action in animals other than the first mentioned.

Strychnine is no longer used in medicine. It causes an increase in sensation. It enlarges the visual field and raises visual acuity so that smaller type can be read. Tactile discrimination becomes greater. In poisonous doses strychnine causes convulsions which are tonic, involving both flexors and extensors. They depend on the arrival of afferent impulses in the spinal cord. Thus in treating strychnine convulsions in a man, he should be moved to a dark and quiet room where he can be given a volatile anaesthetic like chloroform. Strychnine neutralizes the inhibitory action of glycine in the spinal cord.

PURGATIVES, ANTACIDS, ASTRINGENTS, etc.

Constipation

The large intestine is a viscus in which liquid faeces accumulate; water is absorbed and the faeces become solid. Constipation occurs because—

(a) too much water is absorbed so that the faeces become hard;

(b) the solid residue is too small in bulk, and does not distend the intestinal wall sufficiently to make it respond by contraction;

(c) the muscles have insufficient tone.

Constipation can be prevented by

(a) giving more water to drink. This is particularly important in babies who have a large surface area in proportion to body weight, and lose much water through their skin in hot weather;

(b) giving a diet which leaves plenty of indigestible residue; vegetables contain cellulose which remains undigested; brown bread contains bran. The residue can be artificially increased by taking

(1) *bran* (Kellogg's All-bran)

(2) *agar*

(3) *liquid paraffin* (Agarol is a combination of 2 and 3 with phenolphthalein).

(c) taking more exercise. Few of those who do manual work in the open air suffer from constipation. Skipping and horse-riding are particularly effective, perhaps because they promote a free flow of bile.

(d) by taking preparations containing vitamin B_1 (aneurine or thiamine). Some forms of constipation disappear with this treatment.

PURGATIVES AND LAXATIVES

The simplest and least harmful substances are those given to babies and small children.

(a) *Tomato purée* and *spinach purée* are commonly given to babies.

(b) *Dinneford's Magnesia*, a clear solution containing 2·5 per cent $Mg(HCO_3)_2$.

(c) *Milk of Magnesia* or *Cream of Magnesia*, a suspension of hydrated magnesium oxide containing 8·25 per cent $Mg(OH)_2$.

Magnesium chloride (which is formed by interaction of oxide, hydroxide or carbonate with gastric HCl) differs from sodium chloride in that magnesium chloride is not absorbed from the intestine because magnesium ions are not absorbed; thus water is retained in the lumen by osmotic pressure; the water distends the walls of the intestine and increases peristalsis. Purgation then follows. Other substances acting similarly used for adults are—

(d) *Sodium sulphate* (Glauber's salt)

(e) *Magnesium sulphate* (Epsom salts)

The sulphate ion is not absorbed, which explains the action of sodium sulphate. These substances should be given in hypotonic solution as then they act more quickly than in hypertonic solution.

(f) *Grey Powder* consists of 33 per cent mercury and 67 per cent chalk; the chalk maintains the mercury in a fine state of subdivision. Grey Powder owes its action to the mercury, a trace of which is dissolved and stimulates the muscular coats of the small and large intestines. Mercury is also given to adults in the form of

(g) *Calomel*, which is mercurous chloride (dose ½–3 grains). This is a powerful purgative now little used. Mercurous chloride is nearly insoluble but sufficient is dissolved to exert a powerful effect.

Castor oil is a bland oil, only irritant when hydrolyzed. In composition it is the glyceride of a fatty acid, ricinoleic acid;

the fatty acid is set free by the action of the lipase in the duodenum, and the fatty acid exerts the stimulant action on the
small intestine. Castor oil is taken before breakfast, as are
sodium and magnesium sulphate; they act in 1–3 hours.

THE ANTHRACENE PURGATIVES

These comprise cascara, aloes, rhubarb, and senna. All
contain anthracene derivatives combined with sugar as glycoside.
The glycoside is liberated from the drug in the small intestine
and is absorbed into the blood stream. The glycoside is broken
down liberating the active emodin which stimulates the muscular
coats of the *large* intestine in the course of excretion from the
blood. This occurs about 8–10 hours after the drug is taken by
mouth. Hence these purgatives are taken at *night*. These state-
ments have been proved—

(1) by showing that extracts of senna are active when the
small intestine is tied low down in the jejunum so that the
senna cannot reach the large intestine directly;

(2) by showing that extracts of senna are active when
injected into the blood stream;

(3) by showing that extract of senna when injected takes
several hours to act, but emodin when injected acts in
30 minutes.

Senna is perhaps the most widely used of these purgatives.
Four senna pods are soaked in cold water during the day, and
the water is drunk at night. Pleasant preparations are Confection
of Senna, and California Syrup of Figs; Lixen is also pleasant.
Mistura Sennae Co., or Black Draught, is unpleasant, containing
25 per cent $MgSO_4$. Compound Liquorice Powder contains
senna, and is a good purgative for nursing mothers since this
purgative does not affect the baby.

Aloes is similar in action to senna, but stimulates the uterus
as well as the large intestine, and has been known to cause
abortion.

Rhubarb is used as Compound Powder of Rhubarb, or *Pulv.
Rhei Co.* (Gregory's Powder); as it contains tannic acid it reduces
peristalsis when the purgative action is complete.

Cascara comes from the bark of a tree. The extract is commonly prepared as a tablet.

Phenolphthalein is related distantly to the anthracene purgatives. It is widely used to-day in laxative or purgative preparations, some of which are chocolate-coated. It gives rise in susceptible persons to skin rashes, and occasionally causes nephritis. Phenolphthalein is absorbed from the intestine and is taken out of the blood by the liver and is excreted in the bile. Derivatives of phenophthalein follow the same course. Thus *tetra-iodophenolphthalein* is excreted in the bile after being given by mouth or injected intravenously, and if an X-ray photograph is taken it maps out the biliary passages so that the presence of a gall stone can be detected. Compounds containing iodine are radio-opaque because of the high atomic weight of iodine.

Sulphur (brimstone) is given with treacle. In the large intestine sulphides are formed, including H_2S. These stimulate the muscle of the large intestine.

Jalap and **colocynth** are very drastic purgatives which are not now used.

ASTRINGENTS

An astringent is a substance which precipitates protein on the surface of a mucous membrane or elsewhere. There are two classes—heavy metals and vegetable astringents.

Lead acetate is the most widely used salt of a heavy metal. When applied to a raw surface it precipitates protein and forms a skin.

Mercuric chloride might be expected to act in the same way; but the protein precipitate it forms redissolves in excess of mercuric chloride. Thus it corrodes, and is called corrosive sublimate.

Vegetable astringents are:
> **kino,**
> **catechu,**
> **krameria.**

These contain *tannic acid* which is slowly liberated when these substances are taken by mouth. Tannic acid itself cannot be given by mouth since it causes irritation of the gastric mucosa and vomiting. A freshly-made solution of tannic acid is excellent for applying at once to superficial burns or scalds. It forms a skin over the burned area and causes the pain to disappear. It is not suitable for extensive or deep burns.

ADSORBENT POWDERS

Vegetable astringents are used very little to-day to arrest diarrhoea. For this purpose it is usual to give finely divided powders which act by adsorbing toxic substances. For this purpose are used—

Chalk ($CaCO_3$), *Pulvis Cretae Aromaticus,* or aromatic powder of chalk, is commonly used for children.

Kaolin, or china clay, is an aluminium silicate. (Note that aluminium is a non-toxic metal, of lower toxicity than iron. Fears that there is danger in the use of aluminium cooking utensils are entirely without foundation.)

Bismuth carbonate or salicylate line the wall of the intestine and check diarrhoea.

Charcoal also acts as an adsorbent.

ANTACIDS

Antacids are substances used to neutralize excess gastric HCl. The best antacid is *milk*. The next best is **magnesium trisilicate,** which reacts with HCl to form $MgCl_2$; this reacts with $NaHCO_3$ in the intestine to form $MgCO_3$ which is excreted in the faeces. Silicon dioxide is also formed which acts as a coating to an ulcer.

Other commonly used antacids are:

magnesium oxide	3 g.
magnesium carbonate	7 g.
sodium bicarbonate	12 g.
calcium carbonate	7 g.
bismuth oxycarbonate	136 g.

The weights in grammes are the amounts of each needed to neutralize the daily normal output of 1·5 litres gastric juice containing 0·4 per cent HCl. Whereas magnesium oxide and carbonate are laxative, calcium carbonate and bismuth oxycarbonate have the opposite effect. Commonly, mixtures of all four carbonates are prescribed.

Excess use of such mixtures leads to alkalosis in which the plasma bicarbonate is abnormally high and the plasma chloride correspondingly low. The symptoms are those of tetany, muscular twitchings and carpopedal spasm. In extreme forms there may be anuria.

EMETICS AND EXPECTORANTS

These two classes are taken together because, as a general rule, substances which act as expectorants in a small dose act as emetics in a larger dose. Thus Ipecacuanha root is used in the form of **Tincture of Ipecacuanha** (it was formerly called ipecacuanha wine); it is commonly given to small children to produce expectoration by creating the flow of mucus in the bronchial glands. Ipecacuanha stimulates the sensory endings of the vagus nerve in the wall of the stomach. These take impulses to the vagal centre and cause efferent impulses to pass to the bronchial glands. Thus the effect on the bronchial glands is reflex, and not direct. In larger dose, Tincture of Ipecacuanha sends more powerful impulses along the vagal sensory fibres, as a result of which vomiting occurs. Thus ipecacuanha is also a reflex emetic.

Dover's Powder contains 10 per cent opium, 10 per cent ipecacuanha, and 80 per cent lactose. The opium, containing morphine, causes sweating and vasodilatation; it depresses the cough centre; the ipecacuanha increases the flow of mucus in the bronchi and moistens an inflamed mucous membrane. Consequently Dover's Powder is given at bedtime to someone with a feverish cold and a cough.

Other reflex expectorants are:
>   **Tincture of Squills**
>   **ammonium carbonate**

Other emetics are:
>   **mustard in water**
>   **strong sodium chloride solution**
>   **copper sulphate solution**
>   **zinc sulphate solution**

F

Apomorphine is a centrally-acting emetic; it is injected sub-cutaneously and stimulates the vomiting centre in the medulla.

DIRECT EXPECTORANTS

Potassium iodide is the best known member of this class. If a large dose is taken by mouth, it causes a watery secretion of all glands, and the subject feels as if he had a sudden cold in the head. The potassium iodide is itself excreted in these excretions, acting directly on the gland cells.

ACTION OF DRUGS ON THE UTERUS

Pituitary (posterior lobe) extract has been separated into two components—

(*a*) oxytocin

(*b*) vasopressin.

Oxytocin has an action on the uterus, while vasopressin causes a rise of blood pressure on intravenous injection, and has the antidiuretic property.

The main use of oxytocin is in midwifery in which it is used to control post-partum haemorrhage. Its action on the uterus was discovered by Dale in 1909, who observed the potent action on the isolated guinea-pig uterus. The introduction of pituitary (posterior lobe) extract into medicine was due to this discovery. When the baby is born, it remains attached to the uterus by the placenta. The detachment and expulsion of the placenta is the third stage of labour, and during the detachment there is sometimes severe haemorrhage, known as post-partum haemorrhage, because it occurs after the birth of the child. The bleeding is promptly arrested by intramuscular injection of 0·5 ml. oxytocin; since the solution contains 10 units per ml., 0·5 ml. contains 5 units.

A less important use is in the first or second stage of labour before the child is born, to increase uterine contractions and to hasten delivery, when it is given as an intravenous drip. This use is less important because it is dangerous in the hands of the inexperienced. Thus it is essential to be sure that there is no mechanical obstruction to delivery due to (1) defect of the maternal pelvis, (2) disproportion in the size of the baby's head, (3) malpresentation obstructing delivery.

Ergot

Ergot is a fungus (Claviceps purpurea) which grows chiefly on rye (but also on certain grasses, e.g. Festuca grass in New

Zealand). Ergot is in appearance like small purple date stones. Its specific active constituents are ergotamine and ergometrine or ergonovine. These are both derivatives of lysergic acid.

Ergot also contains certain non-specific active principles:

histamine

tyramine

acetylcholine

These are not present in great amount and their presence has no medicinal importance.

Ergotamine has now lost much of its importance since the discovery of ergometrine (ergonovine), but some still remains. Ergotamine causes gangrene by its vasoconstrictor action. This can be demonstrated by injecting it into the breast muscles of a cockerel, after which the comb becomes purple or black in colour due to anoxia. After 2–3 weeks the tips of the comb shrivel and drop off.

In countries where bread is made from rye, epidemics of *gangrenous ergotism* have often occurred due to ergotamine being eaten in the bread. The symptoms begin as a feeling of burning in the extremities; this gave the disease the name of St. Anthony's Fire. The end result was a loss of toes, or even of the whole foot, due to gangrene.

The same symptoms have resulted recently in several cases in which Femergen or Gynergen have been used to treat pruritus (itching). Death has followed. While most patients can take ergotamine without risk, some cannot take more than 2–4 mg. without symptoms occurring.

There is a second form of ergotism due to eating rye bread which is called *convulsive ergotism*. Here the chief symptom is not gangrene, but convulsions, due to an action on the central nervous system. There is also paralysis of extensor muscles. It used to occur in districts where there was very little milk or butter, and where cereals were the main diet. It was known in 1597 that milk and butter prevented it. Mellanby has shown that ergot given in the diet to dogs produces degeneration in the spinal cord if there is a deficiency of vitamin A in the diet, but not otherwise.

Ergotamine has the curious property of converting the constrictor action of adrenaline into a dilator action. Almost all the motor actions of adrenaline are abolished by ergotamine, and some are not only abolished but reversed. Ergotamine causes contraction of plain muscle throughout the body, including the muscle of sphincter pupillae. It has an action on the central nervous system as a result of which the sympathetic system is stimulated, and thus provokes in a cat a condition which has been called sham rage.

Ergotamine is used in the treatment of migraine and of pruritus.

Dihydroergotamine is a derivative of ergotamine which does not produce gangrene. It is used to relieve migraine and for the treatment of headache and *herpes zoster* (shingles)

Ergometrine or Ergonovine

Ergometrine was discovered by Chassar Moir in 1933 and isolated in 1935. In the U.S.A. it is called ergonovine. It is present in watery extracts of ergot, and acts on the uterus within 4–6 minutes of being taken by mouth. It is one of the most rapidly absorbed substances known. Its action on the uterus is the only pharmacological action of importance which it has. It causes a great increase in uterine contractions which persists for 1–3 hours. It does not cause gangrene or have the power of reversing the action of adrenaline. It does, however, cause some sympathetic stimulation by a central action, and in consequence the pupil is dilated.

Ergometrine or ergonovine is used in the treatment of postpartum haemorrhage, when it is given by intramuscular injection.

Syntometrine is a preparation containing oxytocin, 5 units, and ergometrine, 0·5 mg. It is more effective than either alone. Oxytocin is more rapid in action than ergometrine (ergonovine) but ergometrine has a longer duration of action.

THE BLOOD

Metabolism of iron. Iron is required in the body to make haemoglobin. Iron is not excreted in appreciable amounts either in the urine or faeces, and the amount of iron ordinarily found in the faeces is the amount present in the food. Iron is therefore not commonly deficient in men, but it is more commonly deficient in women who lose iron when they lose blood both at the menstrual period and at childbirth. There is an enormous variation in the blood loss of women at menstruation. The only other condition in which iron is deficient is in babyhood, for babies from 2 months up to 2 years of age often have too low a haemoglobin. This is due to receiving too little iron in the diet.

The ordinary intake of iron in the food is about 10–15 mg. a day of which 10 per cent is absorbed. This is not enough for some women so long as menstruation continues and it is not enough in pregnancy. The foods which contain iron are liver, meat, spinach and green vegetables.

Achlorhydria often occurs in iron-deficient anaemia and was thought to be a major cause of failure to absorb iron. It has been shown, however, that addition of HCl to 'labelled' foods does not improve the absorption of radioactive iron, and achlorhydria is now believed to be a consequence of iron deficiency rather than a cause.

Ferrous iron is much more readily absorbed than ferric iron. However, the addition of reducing agents is not very effective in increasing the absorption of iron. Radioactivity studies have also shown that the iron present as porphyrin in the diet, e.g. in myoglobin and haemoglobin, which was formerly thought not to be absorbed, can in fact be absorbed.

McCance and Widdowson have suggested that a mechanism exists to prevent the excessive absorption of iron from the intestine. A patient with hypochromic anaemia absorbs a far greater proportion of orally administered iron than a normal subject. However, the mucosal barrier to the absorption of iron is not absolute. This is well illustrated in the Bantu, where high dietary iron leads to haemosiderosis. There are a number of factors which may enhance or inhibit the absorption of iron from the intestine, e.g. dietary phosphates and phytic acid.

The presence of an iron deficiency can be shown by estimating the iron in the serum, and also the iron-binding capacity of the serum, which is increased when there is a deficiency. Ferrous salts are more effective than ferric salts. Most preparations cause gastric irritation, with diarrhoea or constipation. In many cases these symptoms disappear after the first few days of treatment; a number of patients give up oral iron treatment unnecessarily because of early symptoms of intolerance. Some patients are unable to absorb oral iron, but such cases are rare. They should be given parenteral iron.

The administration of iron. Ferrous sulphate is a satisfactory and economical preparation for the treatment of anaemia due to iron deficiency. Recently organic iron preparations such as ferrous gluconate, succinate and fumarate have been introduced and widely advertised as being more effective and less toxic. A careful comparison with ferrous sulphate has shown that ferrous gluconate and succinate are not appreciably superior to ferrous sulphate, and not appreciably less toxic. Gastrointestinal symptoms (nausea, vomiting, constipation or diarrhoea) appear to be caused by too high dosage. The standard ferrous sulphate tablet contains 60 mg. of iron, and the daily dose does not need to be more than 2–3 tablets. Intolerance to these tablets is in many cases psychological, since in one investigation it was shown that tablets of ferrous sulphate did not induce toxic effects more often than pills which contained only lactose.

There are also chelated iron compounds (one contains the ferric sodium salt of ethylene diamine tetra-acetic acid), but again investigation has shown that they have no great advantage. The organic iron preparations and chelated iron compounds are much more expensive.

Parenteral iron. Some patients, however, are undoubtedly intolerant of iron compounds when given by mouth, and fail to absorb the iron. For these patients *saccharated iron oxide* is given intravenously in doses of 5 ml. containing 100 mg. iron, to a total which may vary from 1 g. to 3·5 g. The injection must be entirely into the vein, for it is irritant if it enters subcutaneous tissues. Reactions occur in about 5 per cent of patients even when no more than 100 mg. iron is given as a single dose. These reactions include a fall of blood pressure, rapid heart and sometimes dyspnoea, cyanosis, vomiting and high fever.

Pernicious anaemia. In microcytic anaemia (also called hypochromic anaemia) the number of red cells is normal, but they are small in size, because there is insufficient haemoglobin to swell them out; in consequence also the haemoglobin value is low, and hence there is too little colour (hypochromic). In pernicious anaemia there is enough haemoglobin but too few red cells. The red cells are swollen (macrocytic) and hyperchromic (having more colour per cell than usual).

Pernicious anaemia was first treated with liver because of Whipple's experiments. He found that when dogs were bled to remove blood, he could influence the rate of regeneration of red cells by various changes in the diet. The most rapid regeneration occurred when the dogs were given liver to eat. Minot and Murphy then gave liver to patients with pernicious anaemia and cured them.

Later, as a result of Castle's experiments, it was found that liver could be replaced by dried hog's stomach and that much less of this was necessary than of liver. Castle suggested that an extrinsic factor in the diet, together with an intrinsic factor in the gastric juice, were necessary for the formation of the haemopoietic factor. The extrinsic factor was eventually isolated as **vitamin B_{12}** or **cyanocobalamin.** It is present in liver, and it is also a growth factor for Lactobacillus dornii. The intrinsic factor is still unknown. It seems to be produced only in the stomach. Since vitamin B_{12} is not absorbed in the absence of intrinsic factor, it is possible that intrinsic factor acts by making absorption possible; or else the intrinsic factor alters vitamin B_{12} to form a complex which is the haemopoietic factor; or else the intrinsic factor is necessary to prevent vitamin B_{12} being taken up by bacteria in the intestine. This last view is supported by the observation that the absorption of vitamin B_{12} given orally is increased by giving an intestinal antibiotic.

Vitamin B_{12} contains cobalt. To patients with pernicious anaemia it must be given by injection; at first 0·25 mg. twice weekly for 3 weeks, then 0·25 mg. weekly until the haemoglobin is normal, and for maintenance 0·25 mg. monthly. The most striking action in patients who are deficient is an immediate feeling of well-being, which occurs long before changes in the blood. This may be because one of the main functions is protein synthesis. In the blood immature red cells appear which contain a reticulum. This can be stained. The cells are called reticulocytes, and may increase until they constitute 20 per cent of the red cell count. This is the 'reticulocyte crisis'. Then they disappear and the red cell count rises rapidly.

Folic acid. The formula indicates that folic acid contains p-aminobenzoic acid as part of the molecule. The history of folic acid is that a substance present in liver and in certain green-stuffs such as lettuce, was observed to be necessary for the growth of the Lactobacillus casei. The substance was isolated and synthesized. Because of its presence in liver, it was tested by giving it to patients with pernicious anaemia (and to other patients with nutritional anaemias characterized as hyperchromic and macrocytic but different from pernicious anaemia), and some patients were cured by folic acid. Later work has shown that folic acid cures nutritional anaemias, but not pernicious anaemia since the neurological symptoms of pernicious anaemia are not improved, and subacute combined degeneration of the spinal cord may occur suddenly during treatment. The relationship between folic acid and vitamin B_{12} is not known.

Phenylhydrazine. This substance and also its acetyl derivative are used when the number of red cells is too great. In polycythaemia the number of red cells may be 10 or 11 million per cub. mm. By giving acetylphenylhydrazine the number can be reduced to 2–3 million.

LEUCAEMIA

When there is an excessive number of white cells in the blood, the condition is called leucaemia, and derivatives of folic acid are used in treatment. **Aminopterin** is obtained by substituting an $-NH_2$ group for an $-OH$ group in folic acid; methotrexate, which is less toxic, has a $-CH_3$ group as well.

Mercaptopurine, a derivative of hypoxanthine, is also used in the treatment of leucaemia. The purines such as hypoxanthine play an important part in the synthesis of nucleic acids. Mercaptopurine prevents nucleic acid synthesis in tumour cells. Another such substance is **azaguanine.**

In treating acute leucaemia in children, mercaptopurine is given first; the disease soon becomes resistant to the drug. Mercaptopurine is then replaced by aminopterin or methotrexate. Finally cortisone or ACTH is given. The combined use of all three treatments may prolong the life of a child by about one year.

Nitrogen mustard, a compound chemically related to mustard gas, is also used in leucaemia, and in Hodgkin's disease. It causes nausea and vomiting. More effective is **triethylene melamine,** which can be given orally.

AGRANULOCYTOSIS

This term indicates a condition, usually provoked by certain drugs, in which the number of polymorphonuclear leucocytes is greatly reduced, so that none can be found at all. Since polymorphs are a most important defensive mechanism, it follows that a patient with agranulocytosis is in extreme danger. The present method of treating agranulocytosis is to withdraw the drug responsible for causing it, and to protect the patient by giving large doses of penicillin to kill bacteria to which he is exposed until the polymorphs return.

Substances causing agranulocytosis

 (1) amidopyrin (an analgesic and antipyretic agent)
 (2) sulphonamides (e.g. sulphathiazole)
 (3) thiouracil (used in treating hyperthyroidism).

All these substances produce agranulocytosis in occasional subjects only, and usually only when the substance has been taken for a long time. One or two cases have been described in which phenacetin has produced agranulocytosis. Phenacetin is the analgesic and antipyretic constituent of Yeast-Vite and of Daisy Powders (taken for headache).

METHAEMOGLOBIN

Some substances have the effect of transforming oxyhaemoglobin to methaemoglobin; this produces some degree of cyanosis. Drugs which do this are:

 (1) sulphanilamide
 (2) sodium nitrite
 (3) acetanilide (analgesic)
 (4) potassium chlorate.

When the blood contains methaemoglobin, the amount can be diminished by injecting methylene blue.

CLOTTING OF BLOOD

 1. Substances which delay clotting are:
  (*a*) sodium citrate, which removes calcium ions
  (*b*) dyes like chlorazol fast pink
  (*c*) heparin
  (*d*) dicoumarol.

Heparin, which can be obtained from liver and is present in most cells, is given by intravenous injection to patients in whom thrombosis has occurred. It prevents or delays coagulation of the blood, its effect lasting for 3–4 hours. It inhibits the conversion of prothrombin to thrombin and neutralizes the action of thrombin.

Dicoumarol is a substance which depresses the formation of prothrombin. It is given by mouth to patients who have first been injected with heparin, to avoid the necessity of repeated injections. As the dicoumarol accumulates in the blood the need for more heparin disappears. The action of dicoumarol is prolonged, and the prothrombin time must be determined daily. There have been many accidents with dicoumarol due to haemorrhage occurring from ulcers and in other places. **Ethyl biscoumacetate** (Tromexan) is a substance similar in action to dicoumarol but safer because it acts for a shorter time.

Warfarin sodium. Whereas dicoumarol (or phenindione, a related substance) can only be given by mouth, warfarin can also be given by intramuscular or intravenous injection. If the prothrombin time becomes too long, it can be reduced by giving vitamin K intravenously.

2. Substances which hasten clotting are:

(*a*) **Russell's viper venom** (Duboia venom) is applied locally to stop haemorrhage in those who suffer from haemophilia (bleeders).

(*b*) **Menaphthone** (menadione or methylnaphthoquinone) is a substance which has the same properties as vitamin K. It increases the production of prothrombin in those deficient. It is commonly given to mothers a day or two before the baby is born, or to the baby just after birth. Haemorrhages also occur in obstructive jaundice because if there is no bile, vitamin K is not absorbed from the intestine and prothrombin then becomes deficient.

3. **Substances which assist fibrinolysis.** John Hunter observed in 1794 that when blood is taken from a man who has died suddenly, either it does not clot at all, or the clot dissolves in 24 hr. The lysis of the fibrin is due to an enzyme *plasmin*, which is normally present in an inactive form *plasminogen*. The plasminogen can be converted to plasmin either by *streptokinase* or by *urokinase*. Streptokinase is present in filtrates of cultures of haemolytic streptococci: it has the disadvantage that it is antigenic since it is not a human protein. Urokinase does not have this drawback, but it is very expensive. These two substances are used in thrombosis to remove blood clot.

USE OF IODINE. THE THYROID

IODINE is used

    (*a*) as iodine itself as a disinfectant

    (*b*) as sodium or potassium iodide in treatment of syphilis

    (*c*) as sodium or potassium iodide as an expectorant

    (*d*) as a radio-opaque substance

        (i) Lipiodol, iodized poppy seed oil, to take a picture of the bronchial tree

        (ii) tetra-iodophenolphthalein for the biliary passages

        (iii) diodone (iodopyracet, Diodrast, Perabrodil, Uroselectan) for the renal pelvis;

    (*e*) as sodium iodide in thyroid conditions

        (i) as a prophylactic against goitre

        (ii) in hyperthyroidism preoperatively (Lugol's iodine).

As a disinfectant iodine is used in solution in alcohol or dissolved in a solution of potassium iodide. It acts very quickly when applied to the unbroken skin, and leaves the surface lethal to any bacteria which may fall on the skin for the next few hours. Iodine is rapidly inactivated in contact with serum or blood (or organic matter in general) and so is not used for wounds. Iodine is absorbed through the skin, and even the vapour of the iodine in a locket tied round the neck may cause a burn of the skin nearby in a sensitive person.

In the treatment of syphilis. In the intervals between periods in which neoarsphenamine is injected, bismuth is given weekly and sodium or potassium iodide daily. In the tertiary form of syphilis, sodium iodide is said to dissolve the mass of fibrous tissue known as the gumma in the centre of which the syphilitic organisms are protected from the arsenical drug.

As an expectorant (see page 73).

As a radio-opaque substance. Iodine, being a substance of high atomic weight, like barium and bismuth, is used for X-ray work, since it is radio-opaque. In addition to the preparations already mentioned, sodium iodide itself has been used for injections into the carotid artery in order that an arteriogram of the head may be taken.

In thyroid conditions. In areas (Derbyshire, Switzerland, around Akron in North America) where iodine is deficient in food and water, large swellings of the neck called goitres, due to enlargement of thyroid gland, are common. The production of goitres occurs as follows. Where there is insufficient iodine in the diet, the thyroid gland cannot make thyroxine. When the thyroxine in the blood falls, the anterior lobe of the pituitary gland becomes active and discharges more thyrotrophic hormone. This stimulates the thyroid gland to grow, and it usually becomes hyperplastic in structure and greatly enlarged.

If sodium iodide is administered at an early stage before the goitre is too big, the goitre diminishes in size and the gland may become normal. If sodium iodide is administered late, the gland regresses a little, but stays big. Colloid is, however, found present in the alveoli, and the goitre is called a 'colloid goitre'.

By giving school children sodium iodide daily for two weeks during four months, the incidence of goitre in Akron was greatly reduced by David Marine.

Sodium iodide in hyperthyroidism. In hyperthyroidism (also known as thyrotoxicosis, Graves' disease, Basedow's disease, or exophthalmic goitre) the symptoms are bulging eyes, swollen thyroid gland seen to pulsate, high pulse rate, high BMR, great nervousness, sweating, tremor, loss of weight.

Until recently all cases which did not spontaneously recover were prepared for thyroidectomy by treating them for two weeks with sodium iodide. Giving sodium iodide daily has the effects of—

(1) reducing the pulse rate
(2) reducing the BMR
(3) increasing the body weight.

The gland ceases to pulsate, thereby becoming less vascular, and it becomes hard. This treatment cannot be continued much

more than two weeks as the condition may suddenly relapse.
Thyroidectomy is then performed. Often Lugol's solution or
Lugol's iodine is given instead of sodium iodide. This contains
5 per cent iodine dissolved in 7·5 per cent solution of potassium
iodide.

MEDICAL TREATMENT OF THYROTOXICOSIS

Thiouracil has been used to treat thyrotoxicosis but it is now
replaced by **methimazole** and **carbimazole** which is given
in daily amounts of 5–10 mg. The introduction of thiouracil
was due to the following curious circumstances. McCollum was
anxious to discover the effect of giving sulphaguanidine to rats.
(Sulphaguanidine was introduced to cure bacillary dysentery
because it was not absorbed, and so killed bacteria in the intestine.)
The discovery was then made that sulphaguanidine caused
enlargement of the thyroid gland in rats, the gland becoming
histologically hyperplastic (the vesicles empty of colloid, and
the cells lining them either cubical or columnar, instead of
being flat as in the resting state). The BMR was found to be
low. Astwood searched for a less toxic substance which would
have the same effect. He found thiourea and thiouracil out of
106 compounds examined. He next demonstrated that thiouracil
arrested the symptoms of thyrotoxicosis in patients.

When taken by mouth thiouracil or its derivatives prevent
the formation of thyroxine by the thyroid gland, so that the
symptoms of thyrotoxicosis disappear, since the symptoms are
due to excess of thyroxine in the blood.

If thiouracil is given to a normal rat, the formation of thyroxine
is reduced as in a patient with thyrotoxicosis. The result is a fall
in blood thyroxine, and, because of this, there is increased
activity of the anterior lobe of the pituitary gland. More thyrotrophic hormone is liberated and in response to it the thyroid
gland enlarges. Hence in the rat thiouracil is sometimes called
a goitrogenic substance. The part played by the pituitary gland
is evident from the fact that if the pituitary gland is removed,
the administration of thiouracil does not cause enlargement of
the thyroid gland.

In patients with thyrotoxicosis, administration of thiouracil does not commonly lead to further enlargement of the gland, but it may do so.

Toxic effects of carbimazole. The toxic reactions are less frequent than those produced by thiouracil; they occur most often within 3–6 weeks of starting treatment. The commonest are itching, erythema and urticaria. More dangerous reactions are very rare; they include agranulocytosis, thrombocytopenic purpura and aplastic anaemia. The drug must be stopped at once, and antibiotics may be given and blood transfusions.

THYROID

The thyroid glands of oxen and of sheep are removed at the slaughter house, and the mass of fat with which each gland is surrounded is cut away. The finer particles of fat are then removed with petroleum ether, and the resulting gland is dried. The material so obtained is called 'thyroid' and is compressed into tablets. It is standardized in terms of the amount of iodine present in organic combination.

Properties:

Taken by mouth it raises the BMR, improves the appetite and makes the patient feel more energetic.

It is used in patients with myxoedema who have a thyroid deficiency, and also in various conditions in which a general stimulation of metabolic processes is desired.

It is often given in obesity, but may make the patient irritable and nervous.

Thyroglobulin is the storage protein of the thyroid gland. It is not the thyroid hormone. Incorporated in it are the active substances thyroxine and triiodothyronine which are released into the blood in the proportion of 9 to 1. The action of triiodothyronine is more rapid but less prolonged than that of thyroxine.

Radioactive iodine. When iodine in the form of potassium iodide, or as a solution of iodine in potassium iodide is given it is very rapidly taken up by the thyroid gland. If the iodine is radioactive, the result is the concentration of radioactive material in the thyroid gland. In hypothyroidism the uptake is very slow; in a normal person it reaches a maximum in 24 hours; in hyperthyroidism in 8 hours. Hence the rate of uptake is used to diagnose abnormal thyroid activity. The uptake is judged by the gamma rays emitted from the skin over the gland. Radioactive iodine can also be used in the treatment of hyperthyroidism, for the β rays emitted by the radioactive iodine in the gland destroy the hyperactive cells. Similarly, radioactive iodine has some value in the treatment of thyroid carcinoma; it causes regression of the tumour cells.

Thyrocalcitonin is a hormone formed in the interfollicular cells of the thyroid gland. It lowers the serum calcium. It antagonizes the action of the parathyroid hormone which causes calcium to leave bone and enter the blood. Thyrocalcitonin causes calcium to go from the blood into the bone (or prevents parathyroid action).

G

DIABETES

DIABETES is treated by:
1. Diet in which carbohydrate is restricted.
2. Administration of oral hypoglycaemic compounds.
3. Administration of insulin by injection.

One-third of all diabetics are controlled by diet only. Those taking oral compounds such as tolbutamide need to have a diet as well, to prevent excessive weight gain. Insulin is needed when oral treatment fails as shown by the occurrence of glycosuria or by a blood sugar which persists over 180 mg./100 ml. blood after a meal. Insulin is also needed when ketosis occurs as shown when blood plasma is tested with Ketostix. Insulin indeed is necessary in the majority of those under 40 who are diabetic but not obese.

Tolbutamide. This substance is a sulphonylurea with the formula:

$$CH_3 \langle\!\!\!\bigcirc\!\!\!\rangle SO_2.NH.CO.NH-(CH_2)_3-CH_3$$

It causes a prompt release of insulin from the pancreas in normal people and in mild diabetic patients. Glucose also has this property of causing a release of insulin from the pancreas, but glucose differs from tolbutamide in that it also stimulates synthesis of insulin, which tolbutamide is unable to do. Hence tolbutamide releases only from preformed stores.

Tolbutamide significantly reduces the fasting blood glucose concentration. It may be that the long-term efficacy of tolbutamide is not so much due to its ability to release insulin as to its ability to reduce the output of glucose from the liver, and to inhibit lipolysis.

Tolbutamide has no useful action in severe diabetes such as is seen in relatively young patients who have ketosis, but a good response may be expected in older, milder diabetics who do not have ketosis. They are often obese.

Tolbutamide has the great advantage that it is taken by mouth.

Different forms of insulin

Insulin has been crystallized, and the current methods of preparing material for clinical use carry it very far on the road to purity. The ordinary soluble insulin so obtained is relatively short-acting, and to obtain a longer-acting substance it is mixed with a protein with which it enters into a loose combination. The protein must, of course, be non-antigenic, and protamine fulfils the requirement. Globin is also used. The combination can be rendered tighter by including a zinc-salt, so that zinc-protamine insulin is still more prolonged in effect than protamine insulin.

	Time to maximum effect	*Time until effect is finished*
Insulin	2–3 hr.	6 hr.
Protamine Insulin .	6–10 hr.	12–18 hr.
Zinc-protamine Insulin	8–15 hr.	24–30 hr.

The advantages of the protamine insulins:

(1) The number of injections is reduced to one per day, especially important for children.

(2) The blood sugar does not rise so high during the night.

(3) Hypoglycaemia is less likely.

The disadvantages:

(1) Since the onset of hypoglycaemia is slow, there is little warning of its occurrence; although it occurs rarely, it is more difficult to counteract than hypoglycaemia due to soluble insulin.

Protamine zinc insulin contains excess protamine which converts a proportion of soluble insulin (when this is added to get an immediate as well as a longer effect) to the long acting form. Isophane insulin does not contain excess protamine. Globin insulin is rarely used now.

OESTROGENIC SUBSTANCES AND STEROID HORMONES

Two naturally occurring oestrogenic substances are

    (1) oestradiol, present in the ovary

    (2) oestrone, occurring in the urine.

These are difficult to obtain pure, and are therefore expensive. The oestrogen most commonly used in medicine is a synthetic substance,

Stilboestrol

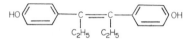

This is active when given by mouth. It is chiefly used at the menopause, when the natural formation of oestrogens is declining, and menopausal symptoms begin to occur, such as sudden hot flushes of the skin of the neck and face, which are embarrassing to the patient. Under the influence of stilboestrol the squamous epithelium normally lining the vagina is restored. Excessive doses cause nausea and vomiting.

Stilboestrol is also used in the treatment of carcinoma of the prostate. This was first successfully treated by removal of the testes; it is now found that giving stilboestrol is equally effective. A small percentage of persons with carcinoma of the breast are also greatly improved, at least for a time.

Dienoestrol has about 60 per cent of the activity of stilboestrol, and **hexoestrol** is still weaker.

Progesterone. The hormone of the corpus luteum is given to patients during pregnancy when previous pregnancies have been terminated by a miscarriage; tablets can be implanted under the skin. Oestradiol causes the uterus of the infantile rabbit to enlarge, but does not cause differentiation of the tissues. If progesterone is injected after the enlargement is induced, the injection causes progestational proliferation of the endometrium.

Contraceptive pills. These at present all contain a mixture of an oestrogen and a progestogen (which is a substance having the properties of progesterone). The day of the onset of menstruation is ordinarily called the first day of the menstrual cycle and the tablets are taken on the 5th to 24th days. The oestrogen is either ethinyl oestradiol or its 3–methyl ether, mestranol. The progestogen is either a 19–norsteroid derivative (such as norethynodrel or norethisterone) or a 17–hydroxy-progesterone derivative. The tablets act by inhibiting the ripening of follicles in the ovary, thus preventing ovulation. The oestrogen plays the dominant role in suppressing ovulation, acting directly on the ovary. The function of the progestogen is to prevent 'break through' bleeding in the mid-cycle and to ensure withdrawal bleeding at the time of the ordinary period.

Rare adverse effects. (1) Jaundice, (2) High blood pressure, (3) Thrombo-embolism. Evidence suggests that thrombo-embolism is determined by the content of oestrogen and this which was generally 100 μg. of (say) mestranol, has now been reduced to 50 μg.; the content of (say) norethisterone remains at 1 mg.

Female infertility. About 15 per cent of females who are infertile owe their infertility to failure to ovulate. The others have surgical or mechanical disorders of the genital tract. Those who fail to ovulate can be treated by injection of human pituitary or menopausal gonadotrophin, followed by chorionic gonadotrophin. They may also be treated by giving *Clomiphene* by mouth. This substance is not a steroid, but is a derivative of ethylene, being a triarylethylene compound. Clomiphene is not oestrogenic. Provided the woman's pituitary gland is capable of producing gonadotrophins, clomiphene has a reasonable chance of enabling her to discharge them in a ratio which will induce ovulation. The urinary output of gonadotrophins should first be estimated, for if they are undetectable, clomiphene does not work. It is said to stimulate an anovulatory ovary to secrete oestrogen, which acts on the hypothalamus with consequent production and release of gonadotrophins. Ovulation follows in 70 per cent and pregnancy in 40 per cent of patients.

SUPRARENAL CORTEX

The suprarenal cortex is deficient in Addison's disease, in which the prominent symptoms are great muscular weakness, pigmentation and low blood pressure. Removal of the suprarenal glands from an animal results in a great loss of sodium chloride from the body and in consequence muscular weakness. This is due to the absence of the hormone aldosterone.

Aldosterone is the natural adrenal hormone which conserves sodium chloride in the body. It increases (1) the reabsorption of sodium by the kidney tubules and (2) the excretion of potassium.

Spirolactones are substances made in the laboratory which neutralize the action of aldosterone. Thus in heart failure, the commonest symptom is oedema. Oedema arises because in heart failure there is increased output of aldosterone (probably because of renal anoxia) and thus increased retention of sodium in the body. Increased retention of sodium means increased retention of water. Therefore there is oedema. When spirolactones are given, the action of aldosterone is neutralized and the oedema disappears. One spirolactone is called aldactone.

Cortisone is the oxidized form of the natural hormone hydrocortisone. It is described as a glucocorticoid because it greatly increases the amount of glycogen in the liver. It was introduced into medicine when it was discovered to remove the symptoms of rheumatoid arthritis. The swelling of the joints rapidly declines and mobility is restored. Its action is not curative.

In general, cortisone reduces manifestations of inflammation; it abolishes fever and lowers the erythrocyte sedimentation rate. Lymphoid tissues are caused to regress and connective tissue growth is suppressed. Cortisone causes a decline in the eosinophil leucocytes in the blood.

The beneficial effects of cortisone in topical skin therapy of lupus erythematosus and pemphigus, in ulcerative colitis, and in asthma are directly due to these anti-inflammatory effects. Thus cortisone is so effective in asthma that it relieves the condition of status asthmaticus in which all other remedies are often useless. Cortisone is also effective in many allergic conditions, such as drug sensitivity. Indeed some kind of allergic response is suspected in rheumatic diseases and in acquired haemolytic anaemia.

But if the cause of disease is bacterial, cortisone may be harmful, because the defence mechanisms are put out of action. Moreover, cortisone is dangerous for long continued use, as peptic ulceration, diabetes, tuberculosis, thrombosis or even psychosis may develop. It causes sodium retention and therefore oedema and the risk of hypertension. It causes loss of calcium.

When cortisone treatment is begun, the secretion of hydrocortisone by the adrenal gland is arrested. Should the patient suffer from infection, trauma or need an operation, his demand for hydrocortisone may then increase from 25 mg. to 100 mg. a day. Unless this increased dose is given he may suffer from an adrenal crisis. This must be treated by intravenous saline and 100 mg. hydrocortisone hemisuccinate. Cortisone is excellent for local application in the eye in conjunctivitis and in iritis. It is used after bilateral adrenalectomy carried out for the treatment of hypertension, Cushing's syndrome and of carcinoma of the prostate. Cortisone is given by mouth.

Hydrocortisone as acetate, hemisuccinate or free steroid is given by intramuscular injection; it has the advantages of freedom from allergic reactions, from difficulties of acquired resistance and from need of close biochemical control. It is the natural hormone liberated from the adrenals when ACTH is given.

Corticotrophin, or **ACTH,** is the hormone from the anterior lobe of the pituitary body which stimulates the activity of the adrenal cortex. There is hypertrophy, and the adrenals are depleted of ascorbic acid and cholesterol. There is increased formation and release of hydrocortisone. Corticotrophin is often found more effective than cortisone; for example, in severe asthma and the other conditions mentioned above. It must be injected, but now that purified preparations are available in a form permitting delayed absorption, it can be given subcutaneously once every day or every other day. It is much cheaper than cortisone.

Dexamethasone, betamethasone and paramethasone have properties similar to those of cortisone and hydrocortisone but differ in not causing sodium retention.

DISINFECTANTS

DISINFECTANTS belong to the following groups:

	Example	*Present in*
1. Halogen derivatives		
(a) Inorganic	NaClO	Dakin's solution
		Milton
	Ca(OCl)$_2$	Bleaching Powder
	Iodine	
(b) Organic	Azochloramid	
	Chloramine-T	
	T.C.P.	
2. Oxidizing agents	H$_2$O$_2$	
	Potassium permanganate	
3. Heavy metals		
(a) Inorganic	HgCl$_2$	
	Mercury biniodide	
	AgNO$_3$	
(b) Organic	Metaphen (mercury)	
	Merthiolate (mercury)	
	Phenylmercuric nitrate	
	Silver proteinate (Argyrol)	
4. Coal tar derivatives	Phenol	
	Cresol	Lysol
	Similar substances	Izal
		Cyllin
	Cl-Xylenol	Dettol
5. Alcohol		
6. Acridine dyes	Proflavine	
	Acriflavine	
7. Other dyes	Gentian violet	
8. Sulphonamides		
9. Penicillin		

1. Halogen derivatives

NaClO and Ca(OCl)$_2$ both release chlorine; this is *very rapid* in disinfectant action: excellent for swimming baths or drinking water. Chlorine, like iodine, is inactivated by organic matter. Hence Dakin's solution if applied to a wound must be applied by irrigation. Iodine is the best disinfectant for unbroken skin but not suitable for wounds.

Organic chlorine compounds like chloroazodine (Azochloramid) liberate chlorine slowly. It is difficult to know how efficient they are.

2. Oxidizing agents

Are rapid in action, but inactivated by organic matter very quickly.

3. Heavy metals

Mercury salts, like mercuric chloride or biniodide, are *very slow* in action, even in high concentration. On the other hand, they kill bacteria in very high dilution if time is allowed. Silver nitrate or proteinate is much used for the eye (in the conjunctival sac). Organic mercurial disinfectants are powerful disinfectants (though not mercurochrome which is inefficient). Can be used for fungus infections, e.g. metaphen for 'athlete's foot' (epidermophytosis).

4. Coal tar derivatives

Phenol, soluble in water, but toxic; causes necrosis if applied to the skin. Has no bactericidal action in a strength less than 0·5 per cent.

Cresol, soluble in soap (Lysol is *Liquor Cresolis Saponatus*), is less toxic, has no action in a strength less than 0·3 per cent.

This class includes Izal, Cyllin, etc.; the action is reduced in the presence of organic matter but not severely. They act more quickly than mercury salts, but still are rather slow.

Dettol is prepared as a liquid and also as a cream containing 33 per cent parachlorxylenol. It is good for wiping on the gloved hands to sterilize them in midwifery.

5. Alcohol

Kills bacteria provided the concentration is about 70 per cent. Alcohol of strength 95 per cent or over has little or no disinfectant action.

6. Acridine dyes

The best of these is proflavine. It is used in a yellow solution 1–1000. Its activity is not diminished by serum or blood, and it is of very low toxicity. (It reduces the activity of leucocytes, however.) Proflavine can be applied to the brain without causing injury. It is an excellent disinfectant for preventing the occurrence of sepsis in a wound, but it is relatively poor against infection once infection is established.

7. Other dyes

Gentian violet is not an acridine dye, but is a mixture of substances which are derivatives of triphenylmethane. It is active against gram-positive bacteria, though the activity is much decreased in the presence of serum.

8. Sulphonamides

These are the first substances to be used successfully to kill bacteria in the body. They have very low toxicity and do not interfere with the action of leucocytes. They are not very successful when applied locally to wounds, but they have some success. They are best against streptococcal infections.

9. Penicillin

Penicillin is ideal as a disinfectant except that it is ineffective against some organisms. Penicillin kills staphylococci as well as streptococci.

DETERGENTS

Various substances known as detergents are being used as soap substitutes. Examples are Cetavlon, Zephyran, Teepol. They lower surface tension, and are excellent for removing grease. They have some disinfectant action, but this is weak. When used for shampoos, they give rise to a severe dermatitis in susceptible individuals.

THE SULPHONAMIDES

THE sulphonamides were discovered in 1935. They represent a landmark in the treatment of bacterial disease; through their agency many diseases such as pneumonia, cerebrospinal meningitis, erysipelas and gonorrhoea have lost a great part of their seriousness.

The sulphonamides were discovered by Domagk who searched for an agent which would protect mice against various infections such as that caused by virulent streptococci. He found *Prontosil*. French workers then showed that the active part of the Prontosil molecule was p-aminobenzene sulphonamide

$$NH_2 \left< \underline{\qquad} \right> SO_2NH_2$$

This became known as *sulphanilamide*.

(Note that it is an aniline derivative.) Other aniline derivatives used in medicine are:

1. phenacetin (analgesic and antipyretic)
2. procaine (local anaesthetic)
3. oxophenarsine or Mapharside (organic arsenical).

Sulphanilamide was first demonstrated to be clinically effective in puerperal septicaemia, a streptococcal infection which until 1936 was of great importance in midwifery. When this disease formerly occurred in a maternity ward, the ward was closed because it was so infectious and had so high a mortality.

Other sulphonamides. The next few years saw the introduction of derivatives of sulphanilamide, of which those in use to-day are

sulphadiazine

sulphadimidine.

How sulphonamides act:

It is generally believed that sulphonamides act by competing with p-aminobenzoic acid for the enzyme which transforms the latter substance into the next product of metabolism. p-aminobenzoic acid is known to be an essential brick in the structure of bacterial cells, and sulphonamides when present in excess prevent it from taking its normal place. If, on the other hand, p-aminobenzoic acid is present in excess, sulphonamides are no longer able to arrest cell growth and multiplication.

Effectiveness of sulphonamides:

This depends on the maintenance of a uniform blood concentration, and it is for this reason that they are given 4-hourly, the patient being awakened at night to receive his dose. The increasing attention which has been paid to the desirability of having a uniform blood concentration of different medicaments (e.g. salicylates, and penicillin) has its origin in the work of Marshall on sulphonamides.

It is usual to aim at a concentration from 6–10 mg. per 100 ml. blood. This is most easily obtained with sulphadiazine and sulphamezathine since these substances are less rapidly excreted.

If sulphonamides are going to be successful they produce an effect quickly, and if no benefit is seen within 2 or 3 days they should be discontinued.

In the body a certain proportion of the sulphonamide given is acetylated and rendered inactive. The proportion may be as little as 10 per cent or as high as 50 per cent. The figure varies with the chemical structure of the sulphonamide and with the patient. Both forms are excreted in the urine.

The effectiveness depends on giving sufficiently large doses at first, and it is better not to give sulphonamides at all than to give doses which are too low, since the organisms then have an opportunity to become resistant.

Toxic effects:

All sulphonamides may produce
   1. Mental depression
   2. Vomiting
   3. Skin rashes
   4. Lumbar pain and haematuria
   5. Agranulocytosis
   6. Drug fever
   7. Methaemoglobin formation and porphyrinuria.

These effects vary greatly in their incidence.

Agranulocytosis is generally confined to patients who are given the drug for too long a time. The period of treatment should not exceed eight days.

Haematuria following lumbar pain is due to the deposition of crystals of the sulphonamide or of its acetyl derivative in the kidney. The occurrence of crystal deposition is minimized by giving the patient plenty of fluid and either sodium citrate or sodium bicarbonate to keep the urine alkaline. If three sulphonamides are used together, as in *Sulphatriad*, only one-third of the amount of each need be used, and the solubility of each is not affected by the presence of the other two. With this combination the risk of crystal deposition is very small.

Skin rashes and drug fever usually stop on withdrawal of the drug.

Sulphonamides for dysentery. There are two forms of dysentery, one due to an amoeba (Entamoeba histolytica) and a second due to various bacilli (Shiga, Flexner, etc.). Bacillary dysentery can be treated by sulphonamides which are not readily absorbed into the blood stream. These are

> phthalyl sulphathiazole (sulfaphthalidine)
> succinyl sulphathiazole.

They can be given in very large doses. They kill the bacteria in the intestine.

Streptotriad is a combination of streptomycin and the three sulphonamides sulphathiazole, sulphadiazine and sulphamerazine. It is very effective in the treatment of bacillary dysentery, particularly in infants, to whom it is given in a dosage of 20 mg. per lb. daily. Adults take 3 tablets at 8 hour intervals for 6 days.

Sulphonamides for urinary infections. When the urinary tract becomes infected, the substances used in treatment are

>   sulphamethizole (Urolucosil)
>   sulphafurazole (Gantrisin)

These are rapidly excreted and very soluble.

Long acting sulphonamides

>   sulphamethoxypyridazine (Lederkyn)
>   sulphadimethoxine (Madribon)
>   sulphamethoxazole (Gantanol)

They are given in doses of one tablet (0·5 g.) per day and when necessary are continued for a month.

Trimethoprim. This is a sulphonamide potentiator, which has the formula

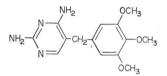

When it is given together with a sulphonamide, the potency of the sulphonamide is greatly increased. Trimethoprim inhibits bacterial dihydrofolate reductases. It thus acts as an inhibitor of the *utilization* of folic acid, while the sulphonamides inhibit the *synthesis* of folic acid. Thus the substance Septrin is prepared in tablets for oral administration which contain 80 mg trimethoprim and 400 mg. sulphamethoxazole. Both substances are antibacterial, but when given together they protect completely in amounts which have no action when given separately.

Septrin is most useful in the treatment of infections of the respiratory and urinary tracts. It is very active against *Haemo-*

philus influenzae, and is also efficient in chronic bronchitis and in *Proteus* infections.

Trimethoprim is readily absorbed by mouth. It shows moderately high binding to serum proteins, and is concentrated in organs to levels several times those of plasma. It is concentrated in the urine.

SODIUM SALICYLATE IN ACUTE RHEUMATIC FEVER

ACUTE rheumatic fever is a disease occurring before the age of 25, in which the chief symptoms are high fever and one or more swollen and painful joints, often the shoulder joint. The disease is difficult to cure, and often leaves behind it damage to the mitral valve of the heart which may incapacitate the patient for the rest of his life. (See p. 111, lines 5 and 6).

Sodium salicylate is the recognized treatment, and this must be given in large doses. It has recently been stated that if the concentration of salicylate in the blood can be raised to 36 mg. per 100 ml., for which amounts of the order of 10 g. daily are required, patients can be more rapidly cured and the risk of heart involvement greatly reduced. The progress of the disease is best discovered by following the sedimentation rate.

Toxic effects of salicylates:

1. Headache, tinnitus, nausea and vomiting.
2. Allergic reactions.
3. Fall in prothrombin in the blood.
4. Hyperpnoea.

Toxic effects are lessened by giving sodium bicarbonate, but this hastens the excretion and thereby lowers the blood concentration. The fall in prothrombin can be compensated by giving menaphthone.

Methyl salicylate is used in the form of a cream for external application. It is useful in lumbago and sciatica, as it is well absorbed through the skin.

THE KIDNEY

THE pH of the urine is usually about 6·0, but may fall to 4·8 or rise to 7·9. The urine is thus usually more acid than plasma (pH $= 7·4$) and this is because sodium ions in the kidney tubule pass into the tubule cells in exchange for hydrogen ions. The hydrogen ions are formed by the dissociation of H_2CO_3 into H^+ and HCO_3^-. The H_2CO_3 is formed under the influence of the enzyme carbonic anhydrase which causes CO_2 to combine with H_2O to form H_2CO_3. Hence the urine will become more acid when more sodium ions are exchanged for hydrogen ions and will become less acid when fewer are exchanged.

To make the urine more acid
ammonium chloride is given by mouth.

If NH_4Cl is given, the NH_4^+ is converted in the liver into urea, and the Cl^- takes some of the Na^+ in the plasma which was balanced by HCO_3^-. Thus the alkali reserve is reduced. The Na^+ and Cl^- are filtered through the kidney glomerulus, and then Na^+ enters the tubule cells in exchange for H^+ which comes out. Thus in effect HCl is present in the lumen of the tubule.

To make the urine more alkaline
sodium citrate (or acetate or tartrate)
or **sodium bicarbonate is given by mouth.**

The citrates or acetates or tartrates of sodium and potassium are converted in the body into carbonates and thus like sodium bicarbonate increase the alkali reserve. Sodium bicarbonate is excreted in the urine, making it more alkaline.

Diuretics

(a) **Hydrochlorothiazide** is a diuretic which is taken by mouth as tablets (up to 100 mg. per day), and which produces a diuresis lasting for 7 to 10 hours. The main effect is to diminish the reabsorption of sodium in the tubules (partly proximal tubules but mainly distal) so that more sodium and therefore more water is excreted. There is also increased excretion of potassium, and if this occurs for a week there are signs of muscular weakness. When giving hydrochlorothiazide it is therefore important to give 2 to 3 g. of KCl per day. A fall in blood potassium is particularly dangerous if the patient is receiving digitalis, for the toxic symptoms of digitalis develop much more easily if the potassium is low. (Toxic symptoms from digitalis are reduced by giving potassium acetate.)

(b) **Bendrofluazide** is similar in action to hydrochlorothiazide, but the dose is one-tenth (10 mg. per day).

(c) **Frusemide** is very potent and has therefore to be used much more carefully; the patient must be watched closely. However it is valuable when it is important to reduce oedema quickly, for example in pulmonary oedema. The dose given by mouth is usually 40 mg. which produces diuresis for 4 hours.

(d) **Ethacrynic acid** is a diuretic which is unrelated to the thiazides, but which is similar in potency to frusemide, that is to say it is capable of achieving diuresis in circumstances in which hydrochlorothiazide would not work. Thus ethacrynic acid can be used effectively when there is a raised blood urea, but its use requires close supervision to guard against low blood pressure caused by a fall in plasma volume.

EXCRETION OF URIC ACID

In gout there is a deposit of uric acid in the joints, and the problems in gout are

1. To arrest the pain of an acute attack. **Colchicine** has long been used for this, but it is being replaced by **phenylbutazone,** which has the advantage that in most cases it causes no gastro-intestinal disturbance. Phenylbutazone is not given to patients with heart disease or with any history of peptic ulceration or blood dyscrasia. Colchicine is a curious substance which can arrest cell division by intervening in mitosis.

2. To increase the excretion of uric acid. This can be done by giving **probenecid** (Benemid) which prevents the tubule

cells from reabsorbing uric acid. (Probenecid was first introduced to diminish the excretion of penicillin by the tubule
cells.) Another substance which prevents the reabsorption of
uric acid is **sulphinpyrazone**.

Allopurinal is an isomer of hypoxanthine. It inhibits the
enzyme xanthine oxidase and therefore reduces the formation
of uric acid.

ANTIBIOTICS

THE term antibiotic was first used to mean antibacterial substances made by moulds.

Penicillin. This is a substance, produced by a mould, which prevents the growth of many bacteria and is at the same time non-toxic. It has been synthesized, but the normal method of production is by fermentation. Penicillin is standardized by comparing each new batch with a standard sample of penicillin G, of which o·6 microgramme is by definition one unit. The test is a test for bacteriostatic action.

Penicillin acts by interfering with the synthesis of the bacterial cell wall, so that large and swollen forms of the bacteria appear. Its effect is bactericidal.

Properties:

(*a*) Very low toxicity.

(*b*) Unstable; it is destroyed when in solution by temperatures over 4° C., by metals, and by other bacteria, which contain an enzyme penicillinase. Solutions should always be freshly prepared.

(*c*) Rapidly excreted by kidney when given intravenously, though its excretion can be reduced by blocking excretion in the tubules with probenicid (Benemid). Does not pass into the cerebro-spinal fluid.

Different forms of penicillin. There are a number of penicillins, which are chemically similar, but have rather different properties. One which is extensively used is *benzylpenicillin*. Its period of action is short so that frequent injections must be given to maintain a high blood concentration. One method of prolonging its action is to use procaine penicillin which is prepared by the interaction of procaine hydrochloride and benzylpenicillin. With this a useful concentration can be maintained in the blood for 12–24 hours.

Another form of penicillin is *phenoxymethylpenicillin* (penicillin V) which is the most satisfactory form of penicillin for oral administration because it is resistant to the acid in the stomach.

A third form is *benzathine penicillin* which maintains an effective blood level for long periods after intramuscular injection. Thus injections given once a month almost completely prevented new infections in rheumatic children.

A compound related to penicillin is *6–aminopenicillanic acid*. A derivative of it is the potassium salt of 6–(α–phenoxypropionamido) penicillanic acid (Broxil) which gives a high concentration in the blood after oral administration.

Penicillinase-resistant penicillins are used against resistant staphylococci. One of these is cloxacillin (Orbenin).

Broad spectrum penicillins; one of these is ampicillin (Penbritin).

Streptomycin is an antibiotic obtained from the mould *Streptomyces griseus*, which also is a source of vitamin B_{12}. Its most important use is in tuberculosis. Streptomycin is given by intramuscular injection, because it is poorly absorbed from the gut. However, it is not inactivated in the gut, and can be given by mouth to exert a local action in the gut. When streptomycin is given intramuscularly, very little enters the cerebrospinal fluid. However, it can be given intrathecally for the treatment of tuberculous meningitis and effective levels are maintained for 30 hours.

When streptomycin is given alone in the treatment of tuberculosis, the organisms rapidly become resistant to its action. There are, however, two other agents which kill tubercle bacilli, which are isoniazid and p–aminosalicylic acid. When both these substances are given together with streptomycin, then resistance does not develop. The usual treatment, therefore, is to give streptomycin 1 g. daily, isoniazid 0·1 g. twice daily and p–aminosalicylic acid, 5 g. three times daily. When patients are over 40 years of age, they are given streptomycin not more than three times a week because of the risk of damage to the vestibular nerve.

Other antibiotics useful in tuberculosis are **viomycin** and

cycloserine. They are, however, less active than streptomycin and more toxic.

Chloramphenicol was the first antibiotic which was found to be curative in a rickettsial infection; it was found to cure typhus. Since then it has been found to cure typhoid fever and also whooping cough. It is well absorbed when given by mouth. It diffuses very easily in the tissues and probably reaches a higher concentration in the tissues than many other antibiotics. Its beneficial action in typhoid may depend on its ability to diffuse, since outside the body chloramphenicol is not more active against typhoid than are the tetracyclines, but in the body the tetracyclines are not effective.

Tetracyclines. There are three substances. The first is chlortetracycline (aureomycin), oxytetracycline (terramycin) and tetracycline. They are usually given in capsules by mouth. They are often described as 'broad-spectrum' antibiotics because they are effective against a wide range of bacteria and not so specific.

Erythromycin is useful against staphylococci which are resistant to penicillin, and generally when other antibiotics are ineffective. It should be kept in reserve. It is given orally, but can be injected.

Polymyxin (B or E) is a polypeptide which is useful in the treatment of infections with *Pseudomonas pyocyanea*. All strains of this gram-negative organism are killed by low concentrations of this antibiotic. Since infection with this organism is otherwise very difficult to treat, polymyxin has an important therapeutic use. It is also effective against other gram-negative bacilli in the urinary tract or in wounds.

Cephaloridine is an antibiotic which acts against staphylococci which are resistant to penicillin as well as to those which are sensitive to penicillin. It is bactericidal, and not merely bacteriostatic. Cephaloridine is active against both gram-positive and gram-negative organisms and is non-toxic. It is poorly absorbed by mouth and must be given by injection. It is useful in treating patients with acute pyelonephritis because of its low toxicity.

Action of penicillin. Penicillin is toxic to gram-positive bacteria, but has little action on gram-negative bacteria, and is without effect on animal, plant, protozoal and fungal cells. Penicillin acts by preventing the normal growth of the bacterial cell wall, by interfering with the synthesis of wall substance. Thus it acts only on growing cells. Such cells in the presence of penicillin become unusually large, even spherical, and have abnormal shapes. On account of the absence or abnormality of the cell wall, they are very sensitive to changes in osmotic pressure outside them.

Bacitracin, which is another antibiotic, is a polypeptide, and acts in a similar way to penicillin, preventing the synthesis of the wall substance. Both penicillin and bacitracin also have some effect in preventing the incorporation of amino-acids into the bacterial cell protein.

Chloramphenicol inhibits the synthesis of protein by the bacterial cell, doing so without any obvious inhibitory action on RNA synthesis. Tetracyclines act in a similar way.

Bacterial resistance to antibiotics. The more antibiotics are used the less useful they are likely to become in the treatment of certain common infections especially those caused by the staphylococci, the gram-negative bacilli and by *Mycobacterium tuberculosis*. This is because of the emergence of resistant strains. However, it is fortunate that this is not true for the *Treponema pallidum* of syphilis, for *Streptococcus pyogenes*, the pneumococcus, the gonococcus, the meningococcus or for *Clostridium welchii*. Moreover, in the same bacterial species, resistance emerges readily towards some drugs, but not to others.

Often more than 80 per cent of the staphylococci isolated to-day from patients in hospital are resistant to penicillin, and at least half as many are resistant to the tetracyclines. A variable proportion are resistant to streptomycin, chloramphenicol, erythromycin and even to novobiocin.

Resistance to penicillin depends mainly on the formation of an enzyme penicillinase which destroys penicillin. This is at least true of those resistant organisms which are found in infections. There are two ways in which resistant bacteria may replace sensitive bacteria; the strain originally present in the patient may become resistant or the lesion may be secondarily colonized by resistant bacteria which are present in the environment.

Resistance to an antibiotic (streptomycin, the tetracyclines, chloramphenical, erythromycin and novobiocin) emerges readily in hospitals where much of that antibiotic is used. However, **vancomycin** and **ristocetin** do not appear to induce the emergence of resistant staphylococci.

Fortunately the problem of antibiotic resistance has not led to an increase in the death rate from infective disease. The deaths, including those from tuberculosis, show a continuous decline.

Dangers of antibiotic treatment. The most serious danger of antibiotic treatment is an anaphylactic reaction resulting in death, which has followed the injection of **penicillin** more commonly than it has followed the injection of other antibiotics. Therefore an inquiry should be made whether there have been allergic reactions to penicillin on any previous occasion. Skin reactions vary from mild erythema to exfoliative dermatitis.

When penicillin is given by mouth, there may be heartburn, nausea and diarrhoea.

Streptomycin also produces allergic reactions, but the most serious effect is on the VIIIth nerve. There may be damage to the cochlear and also to the vestibular portions, the risk being greater in older subjects. Streptomycin should not be given more often than three times weekly to those over 40 years of age. The risk of damage to the VIIIth nerve depends on the length of time streptomycin is given.

Tetracyclines are dangerous because in their presence there may be an overgrowth of *Candida albicans* in the gastro-intestinal, respiratory and genito-urinary tracts. This results from the depression of the normal bacterial flora. In extreme cases there may be a fatal septicaemia due to monilia. The second danger which may arise during the use of tetracyclines is an infection with resistant staphylococci picked up in the hospital environment. This may cause severe and sometimes fatal entero-colitis.

Indications for use of antibiotics. It is important to identify the infecting organism, and then to choose the antibiotic to which it is most sensitive. A raised temperature or a cold or sore throat is not an indication for an antibiotic. Antibiotics are substances of large molecular weight and diffuse poorly through the pleura, the peritoneum and the pericardium. To treat a pleural abscess, injection should be made into the pleural cavity. Antibiotics do not pass through the meninges of healthy persons, though a little may pass through inflamed meninges. They should not be expected to pass through an abscess wall, and the abscess must first be treated surgically.

ORGANIC ARSENICAL COMPOUNDS

THE simplest organic arsenical compound is **oxophenarsine** (Mapharside).

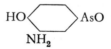

The arsphenamines were discovered by Ehrlich in Germany as a result of experiments on animals infected with trypanosomes, followed by experiments on spirochaetes related to *Treponema pallidum* which is the causal organism of syphilis. Trypanosome infections generally respond, in greater or less degree, to the same drugs as spirochaete infections. An exception is penicillin, which acts on spirochaetes but has no action on trypanosomes.

The use of the trivalent arsenical compounds (such as oxophenarsine) for syphilis has now given place to the use of penicillin, but the pentavalent arsenicals are still used.

Tryparsamide

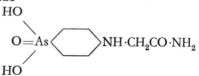

Is used in tertiary syphilis or neurosyphilis because it penetrates the central nervous system. For this reason it is also the best drug commonly used for the late or cerebral stage of sleeping sickness due to infection by trypanosomes. It may cause optic neuritis, and should then be withdrawn.

Carbarsone is another pentavalent arsenical used in amoebic dysentery.

Mel B which contains both phenylarsonic acid and dimercaprol is used in the treatment of trypanosomiasis. The dimercaprol reduces the toxicity of the arsenic to the host more than to the parasite.

Dimercaprol was discovered in an attempt to find an antidote to lewisite, an arsenical war gas which burns the skin. It was found to be able to remove a burn produced by lewisite. The two –SH groups combine with one atom of arsenic.

In treating exfoliative dermatitis which arises sometimes when treating patients with neoarsphenamine, dimercaprol is given by intramuscular injection in peanut oil. The arsenic in the skin which is responsible for the dermatitis combines with the dimercaprol and is removed. The dermatitis heals in a few days instead of taking several weeks. Dimercaprol is also of value in mercury poisoning, because mercury, like arsenic, combines with –SH groups. It is also of use to treat symptoms produced by other metals such as gold. Thus sodium gold thiosulphate is used in treating rheumatoid arthritis, and sometimes it produces intensely painful conjunctivitis.

MALARIA

by L. G. Goodwin

IT MIGHT BE considered that malaria and other tropical diseases are of little importance in Britain. This is not so. The jet aeroplane now carries millions of passengers into and out of the tropics every year, well within the incubation periods of the diseases that may be encountered before returning to temperate regions. At least forty severe cases of malaria (mostly diagnosed post mortem) occur in Britain every year.

Malaria is a disease caused by a parasite of which there are several species (e.g. *Plasmodium vivax*, *Plasmodium falciparum*) which is carried by the mosquito. The parasites exist as sporozoites in the salivary gland of the mosquito. When the mosquito bites, sporozoites are introduced into the man's blood, but they disappear quickly and no more is seen of them for about 10 days. During this time they are multiplying in the cells of the liver. Then they reappear in the red cells as trophozoites and multiply there. The schizonts so formed burst the red cell in about 48 or 72 hours depending on the species of parasite and then the fragments of these schizonts, known as merozoites, invade other red cells where they become trophozoites again and the whole cycle is repeated. Fever occurs when the schizonts burst the red cells, at intervals of 48 or 72 hours. While this process of schizogony is going on, gametocytes of both sexes are formed. These do not conjugate in man, but only in the body of a mosquito which has fed on an infected man. After a cycle of development in the mosquito the parasites reach its salivary glands as sporozoites, and the mosquito is infective for man.

The malaria parasites in the liver cells are known as exo-erythrocytic forms. The exoerythrocytic form during the 10-day interval between the sporozoites and the first appearance of trophozoites in the blood is known as the pre-erythrocytic form. The exo-erythrocytic parasites are very important in the chemotherapy of malaria because they are much more resistant to treatment than the red cell forms.

The exo-erythrocytic parasites of *P. vivax* continue to multiply in the liver and to infect other liver cells. They may lie dormant for months at a time and that is why people who leave the tropics with this infection (benign tertian malaria) may continue to have attacks of fever long after they have ceased to be exposed to malaria. The exo-erythrocytic forms of *P. falciparum* (malignant tertian malaria) are short-lived; they pass from the liver cells into erythrocytes and do not infect other liver cells.

The drugs used in the chemotherapy of malaria are classified according to their actions as:

Blood schizontocides—that kill asexual parasites in the blood and therefore terminate acute attacks and, if taken regularly, suppress malarial infections.

Tissue schizontocides—that kill parasites in the liver cells and therefore cure *P. vivax* infections.

Gametocytocides—that kill sexual parasites in the blood and prevent transmission to the mosquito vector.

Chloroquine (Nivaquine) was discovered by the Germans as 'resochin' but was tested and developed in America during the last war. It is a derivative of 4-aminoquinoline and is a blood schizontocide. It kills asexual parasites in the erythrocytes but has no effect on exoerythrocytic forms. Chloroquine is used for the treatment of acute malarial fever and also for preventing the occurrence of attacks. This is called suppression because the drug does not kill the sporozoites which the mosquito introduces, nor the pre-erythrocytic forms in the patient's liver; it acts on the trophozoites as they emerge from the liver cells and prevents them from parasitizing the red cells.

The suppressive dose of chloroquine is 300 mg. (base) once weekly and this must be taken regularly throughout the time spent in malarious areas. If continued for 3–4 weeks after leaving the area, all the exoerythrocytic forms of *P. falciparum* will by then have completed their development and will have been killed by the drug. *P. vivax*, on the other hand, may remain alive in the liver cells and the infection may recrudesce later on.

Amodiaquine (Camoquin) is also a 4-aminoquinoline compound with action and uses similar to those of chloroquine.

Quinine was for many years the only effective drug for malaria. It is one of the alkaloids found in cinchona bark and, like the other cinchona alkaloids (quinidine, cinchonine and cinchonidine) is a blood schizontocide. The usual suppressive dose is 300 mg. daily but this is not always sufficient to give full protection. Larger doses cause unpleasant effects such as ringing in the ears, deafness and visual disturbance (cinchonism) and if quinine is taken irregularly, acute haemolytic attacks called blackwater fever may occur. For these reasons quinine has been replaced by less toxic suppressive drugs.

It still finds an important place in the treatment of infections with strains of parasite that are resistant to other drugs. It is also used in the treatment of cerebral malaria because it acts so rapidly when given by intravenous injection.

Primaquine is an 8-aminoquinoline derivative. It has little action on asexual blood parasites but is an excellent tissue schizontocide. It is therefore used for the radical cure of *P. vivax* infections in people who are leaving the tropics. For this purpose it is given in doses of 15 mg. (base) daily for 14 days. Weekly doses of 45 mg. (base) are also given, together with a suppressive dose of chloroquine (300 mg. base) in areas of the Far East where *P. vivax* is common and causes most trouble.

Primaquine is also a gametocytocide and is sometimes used together with chloroquine in malaria control programmes when it is important to reduce the hazards of renewed transmission by mosquitos.

Primaquine causes haemolysis and methaemoglobinaemia in human races with genetic deficiency of glucose-6-phosphate dehydrogenase in the erythrocytes.

Proguanil (Paludrine) is a biguanide derivative. It is a blood schizontocide. It also has some action on pre-erythrocytic parasites and reduces the infectivity of gametocytes to the mosquito. Proguanil is an effective suppressant when taken in doses of 100 mg. daily.

Chlorproguanil is closely related to proguanil but is more potent. It is given in weekly doses of 20 mg.

Cycloguanil (Camolar) is the metabolite into which proguanil is coverted in the body. Its activity is short-lived but if injected in oily suspension as an insoluble salt, is released slowly over a long period. It has been used as a long-acting suppressant in control campaigns.

Pyrimethamine (Daraprim) is related to cycloguanil. It has similar actions but is more potent and is given once weekly in doses of 25 mg. It is also used together with chloroquine to prevent renewed mosquito transmission in control campaigns.

Proguanil and its relatives are inhibitors of dihydrofolic reductase enzymes and interfere with the nuclear division of malarial schizonts. They are strongly potentiated by sulphones such as dapsone and by long-acting sulphonamides, which also have antimalarial activity of their own by virtue of their competition with *p*-aminobenzoate.

In some areas strains of malaria parasites exist that are resistant to antimalarial drugs. Strains resistant to proguanil and pyrimethamine are usually sensitive to chloroquine. Resistance to chloroquine is uncommon but is encountered in parts of Southeast Asia and South America. Fortunately such infections are usually sensitive to quinine, or to pyrimethamine given with sulphone or sulphonamide.

OTHER TROPICAL INFECTIONS

AMOEBIC DYSENTERY

THIS form of dysentery is due to *Entamoeba histolytica* which lives in the large intestine. The amoebae devour the cells of the mucous membrane and cause large, bleeding ulcers with undermined margins. Sometimes amoebae are carried in the portal blood to the liver where they cause amoebic hepatitis or liver abscess. The disease has long been treated with ipecacuanha root, the active principle of which is emetine, but a wide variety of synthetic drugs has also been used.

Emetine, as its name implies, is a powerful emetic when given by mouth. Small doses cause salivation and bronchial secretion. In the treatment of dysentery the hydrochloride is injected subcutaneously for 10 days, but not for longer as it may produce toxic effects, especially on the heart. It acts on the motile form of the parasite and rapidly controls acute amoebic dysentery; it is rarely successful in producing a complete cure if given only by injection. This is because parasites living in the lumen of the gut are not reached by the drug in the tissues of the host.

Emetine and bismuth iodide can be given in capsules or tablets by mouth without causing vomiting, and is used to follow a course of emetine injections. It kills amoebae in the lumen of the bowel which escape the action of the drug given by injection.

Emetine is stored in the liver and it is effective against amoebae which are swept by the bloodstream into the liver and give rise to amoebic hepatitis or liver abscess. The antimalarial drug chloroquine is also used for the treatment of amoebic hepatitis.

Dehydroemetine has an action similar to that of emetine.

Metronidazole (Flagyl) is a nitroimidazole derivative, first introduced for the oral treatment of *Trichomonas vaginalis* infections of the urogenital tract. It was later found to have a powerful effect on *E. histolytica* and as it is less toxic than emetine, is now widely used in the treatment of amoebic dysentery. The dose is about 1·2 g. daily for 5–10 days.

Other substances used alone, or in various combinations for the treatment of amoebiasis are:

Acetarsol and **carbarsone:** sparingly soluble pentavalent arsenicals, given by mouth in chronic infections.

Diodoquin, chiniofon and **clioquinol:** iodinated hydroxy-quinoline derivatives, given by mouth or as an enema.

Diloxanide, clefamide and **chlorbetamide:** acetamide derivatives, given by mouth in chronic infections.

Niridazole, introduced for the treatment of schistosomiasis, also has useful activity against amoebic infections.

SLEEPING SICKNESS

This disease is due to trypanosomes, and occurs in Africa, where it is transmitted by tsetse flies. There are two stages of infection: early, in which the blood and lymphatic systems are involved; and late, in which the trypanosomes have reached the brain and cerebrospinal fluid. Infections with *Trypanosoma gambiense* are more widespread and more chronic than those with *T. rhodesiense,* which often appears as localized outbreaks of acute disease. There is no morphological difference between the two species. The early stages of the disease are treated by injections of **pentamidine,** an aromatic diamidine, or of **suramin** (also known as Bayer 205, Antrypol or Geruanin). The late stage of the disease requires a drug that will penetrate to the central nervous system and is usually treated with injections of **tryparsamide.**

Better results are obtained with the melamine derivative **Mel B** (Arsobal) which is a compound of melamine, phenylarsonic acid and dimercaprol (BAL). The dimercaprol has the action of detoxicating the arsenic. This action is less pronounced on the toxicity of the drug to the parasite than to the host and

I

therefore larger and more effective doses of arsenic can be given. The compound **Melarsen,** which contains melamine and arsenic but no dimercaprol, is used in the treatment of early trypanosomiasis.

Inadequate treatment results in the development of drug resistance. Tryparsamide-resistant trypanosomes are usually sensitive to Mel B, but Mel B-resistant trypanosomes are resistant to all known drugs except **nitrofurazone,** which often causes unpleasant side-effects.

Pentamidine and suramin are both retained in the body for weeks or months after injection, and so they are useful prophylactic agents. In some parts of Africa sleeping sickness has been controlled by giving *everyone* (which may mean many thousands of people) in a selected area one or two prophylactic injections of pentamidine, so that no one can become infected. The life of a tsetse fly is shorter than the duration of the protection, so that by the time the prophylactic action is over, the infected flies have been replaced by their uninfected offspring, and the whole area should then be free from the disease. It is important in such schemes of mass-treatment to ensure that all people already having trypanosomes in their central nervous systems are adequately treated with arsenic. Otherwise the infection may progress to an advanced stage while the blood and lymph remain free from trypanosomes as a result of the treatment with pentamidine.

There is a further snag, in that game animals and cattle may harbour trypanosomes that infect man and may therefore act as reservoirs of the disease.

Another form of trypanosomiasis is found in South America and is caused by *T. cruzi*. It is transmitted by large bugs and is called Chagas's disease. It causes serious damage to the muscles of the heart and the alimentary tract; there is as yet no satisfactory treatment.

Trypanosomiasis of cattle is economically more serious to man than the infection of man himself. The most common species in cattle, *T. congolense* and *T. vivax*, are not cured by the drugs used against human sleeping sickness. They are treated with **quinapyramine** (Antrycide), **diminazene** (Berenil) or **isometamidium,** a phenanthridinium derivative.

LEISHMANIASIS

The disease is caused by protozoan parasites of the genus *Leishmania* which are related to the trypanosomes and are transmitted by sandflies. There are two main forms of the disease, a generalized, usually fatal infection known as kala-azar (*L. donovani*) and a skin ulceration known as oriental sore (*L. tropica*). These diseases are still quite common in Africa, India and the Mediterranean littoral. Other forms of leishmaniasis, causing disfiguring facial muco-cutaneous lesions (*L. brasiliensis*) or ulcers on the ears (*L. mexicana*) are found in South and Central America. Wild animals act as reservoirs of all forms of the disease.

Tartar emetic (potassium antimonyl tartrate), or the equivalent sodium salt, is the cheapest form of treatment. When injected it must be given intravenously because it is highly irritant to subcutaneous tissues. It is the best known antimony compound. As its name implies, when given by mouth it acts as an emetic, and a few centuries ago its use became so widespread as a treatment for many diseases that it became a scandal. Doctors had to promise the University of Paris that they would not use it, before receiving a degree. Pentavalent organic antimonials such as **sodium stibogluconate** (Pentostam) are much less toxic and have replaced the trivalent compounds for the treatment of leishmaniasis.

LEPROSY

Leprosy is caused by a bacillus related to the tubercle bacillus. For 100 years it was treated by **chaulmoogra oil** and **hydnocarpus oil,** but **dapsone** (diamino-diphenyl sulphone) is now the standard drug for the treatment of leprosy. It is given by mouth in doses of 25–200 mg. twice weekly and treatment must be continued for several years.

Thiambutosine, a derivative of phenylthiourea, is used for patients who cannot tolerate sulphones. **Ditophal** (diethyl dithiol isophthalate) is rubbed into the skin and produces its effect by hydrolysis to ethyl mercaptan, a foul-smelling volatile liquid. Leprosy bacilli develop resistance to ethyl mercaptan fairly rapidly and therefore dapsone or thiambutosine are usually given concurrently.

Inoculation against tuberculosis with BCG affords significant protection against leprosy also; there is now a hope that this ancient disease may be brought under control.

WORM INFESTATIONS

MOST people in the world are infected with worms. For example in Egypt ten million people, or nearly 70 per cent of the population, suffer from schistosomiasis. And they have most of the other worms there as well. The three main classes of parasitic worms are:

Cestodes (from *kestos,* a girdle)—tapeworms.
Trematodes—flukes, the most important of which are the human blood-flukes or schistosomes.
Nematodes—which include: Roundworms (*Ascaris*), Threadworms or pinworms (*Enterobins*), Hookworms (*Ancylostoma* and *Necator*), Filarial worms (*Wuchereria* and *Onchocerca*).

Roundworms and threadworms are universal; hookworms occur mainly in the tropics and filarial worms exclusively in tropical areas.

Tapeworms

The drug most commonly used for the removal of tapeworms is **Niclosamide,** a salicylamide derivative. A dose of 1 g. is given on an empty stomach, followed by a second dose of 1 g. an hour later. No purging is necessary. The worm is normally partly digested when passed and it is difficult to identify the scolex.

Dichlorophen has a similar action; doses of 6 g. are given on each of two successive days. This drug causes diarrhoea and sometimes vomiting, which is undesirable in tapeworm infestations because if segments of the worm containing viable eggs pass into the stomach it is possible for them to hatch, invade the host and cause cysticercosis.

Mepacrine (the antimalarial drug) is also an effective treatment for tapeworms but the large dose used (0·8 g.) often causes vomiting.

Extract of Male Fern (**Aspidium filix-mas**) is an old-fashioned but effective remedy. The patient is put to bed and is given a purge and a light diet for the day. The next morning the liquid extract of male fern is given, to be followed in 2–3 hours by a saline purge to remove the extract of male fern. If this stays in the intestine and is absorbed it produces toxic symptoms. The use of castor oil as a purge aids the absorption of the filicic acid in the extract of male fern; hence a saline purge, e.g. magnesium sulphate, is used. The head of the worm must be identified in the patient's stools, for if it remains in the intestine the worm will grow again.

Schistosomes

Schistosomes (or Bilharzia worms) live in the small veins of the intestine and bladder. In *Schistosoma mansoni* infections the paired male and female worms migrate to the intestinal vessels; eggs are laid and these penetrate the wall of the gut and are excreted in the patients' faeces. *S. haematobium* lives in the vesical plexuses and the eggs penetrate the bladder wall and appear in the urine. Both of these species are common in Africa and South America. A third species, *S. japonicum*, inhabits all the visceral organs. It is found in the Far East. Apart from the damage and loss of blood caused by the passage of schistosome eggs through the tissues, eggs that enter the blood stream are washed back into the liver by the portal flow and cause severe tissue reactions and cirrhosis.

Tartar emetic is used by intravenous injection. It is effective but the course is long and side reactions—cough, vomiting and damage to the myocardium—are severe.

Sodium antimonyl gluconate (Triostam), **stibophen** and **stibocaphate** (Astiban) are also organic derivatives of trivalent antimony and are less toxic than tartar emetic.

Lucanthone (Miracil D, Nilodin) is a thioxanthone derivative with activity against *S. haematobium* when given by mouth.

Niridazole (Ambilhar) is a nitrothiazole derivative that is effective on all species of schistosome when treatment is given by mouth. Side-effects in children are rare. In adults who, because of hepatic cirrhosis of long standing, have developed vascular connexions between the portal and systemic circulations, the drug by-passes the liver and causes psychiatric disturbances. The organophosphorus insecticide **Trichlorophon** (Dipterex) is useful for the treatment of *S. haematobium* infections and although the drug is an inhibitor of cholinesterase, side-effects are not severe.

The life cycle of schistosomes includes an essential phase in fresh-water snails, so that if the snails could be destroyed the infection would disappear from an infected area. In practice, molluscicides have not proved very successful, due to the difficulty of spraying all breeding-sites and the rapidity with which snails recolonize an area when the effect has worn off. These drugs have had some influence in rigidly controlled irrigation schemes.

Threadworms

Threadworms (Enterobius) are the commonest infestation in temperate climates, particularly among children. They live in the lower part of the large intestine and in the rectum. The female worms creep out of the anus at night to lay their eggs, and this sometimes makes children scream. Syrup or tablets containing preparations of **piperazine** are used. The whole family is usually infected although all may not show symptoms. It is therefore important to treat both parents and children.

Viprynium (Vanquin), an orange-red dye and **Gentian violet** are also used for expelling threadworms.

Roundworms

Ascaris lumbricoides is a large worm, looking superficially like the common earthworm. Males and females live in the lumen of the small intestine; the females each lay about 300,000 eggs a day. Like threadworms, they are treated very effectively with **piperazine,** which narcotizes them. They are unable to maintain their position in the gut and are swept out with the contents of the bowel. **Santonin** is also used; it is given with calomel at night, followed by a saline purge in the morning. Santonin is toxic when it is absorbed, and the presence of fat or oil in the intestine assists this. Santonin then causes yellow vision; in larger doses it causes vomiting and diarrhoea, and sometimes convulsions.

Oil of chenopodium and **hexylresorcinol** (by mouth) are also used for ascaris infections.

Thiabendazole has a powerful action on most parasitic nematodes of man and domestic animals; it is effective against roundworms, threadworms and hookworms.

Hookworms

Ancylostoma and *Necator* live attached by their teeth to the walls of the duodenum. They are small and threadlike but are sometimes found in enormous numbers and, as they feed on blood which they suck from the mucosal vessels, may cause severe anaemia.

The cheapest treatment for hookworms is **tetrachloroethylene.** Although it is a chlorinated hydrocarbon and is unpleasant to take, the drug has remarkably few toxic side-effects and can be given with, or without, a purge. **Bephenium** (Alcopar) is bitter, but more pleasant than tetrachloroethylene and is particularly effective on *Ancylostoma* infections. Thiabendazole and the veterinary anthelminthic, **Tetramisole** are also used.

Filarial worms

The adult forms of the most widespread species, *Wuchereria bancrofti,* live in the lymphatics and, by blocking them, cause elephantiasis. Every night a swarm of immature worms (or larvae) invades the blood stream, and then mysteriously disappears at dawn. Mosquitoes transmit the infection by feeding on blood containing these larvae. A piperazine compound, **diethylcarbamazine** (Hetrazan or Banocide), destroys the larvae, and has some action on the adults, especially during the early stages of the disease.

A serious form of filarial infection in Africa, causing blindness, is *Onchocerca volvulus,* which is transmitted by a small biting fly called *Simulium damnosum*. Diethylcarbamazine is active also against this infection, but must be given with caution because the liberation of foreign protein from dead worms frequently causes sensitization reactions which may do more damage to the eyes than that caused by the worms. Antihistamine drugs and cortisone may be used to reduce the severity of the reaction. The trypanocidal drug suramin (Bayer 205) is also used in the treatment of onchocerciasis.

SKIN CONDITIONS

Scabies is due to a mite which burrows in the skin. It is treated with **sulphur ointment** (one application only should be made or else a dermatitis is produced); or with **benzylbenzoate** which is applied with a brush; or **Tetmosol soap** (Tetmosol is tetraethylthiuram monosulphide).

Ring worm (Tinea capitis) responds well to oral treatment with antibiotic **Griseofulvin** (also used for ringworm of glabrous skin which does not respond to fungicidal lotions or salves).

Lice can be killed by a powder containing **dicophane** (or DDT), which is dichlorodiphenyltrichloroethane. This is likewise lethal for bugs, flies, etc. **Gamma benzene hexa-chloride** (Gammexane) is also useful for this purpose. It is the gamma isomer of benzene hexachloride. Both dicophane and gamma benzene hexachloride are insoluble in water, but they form fine aqueous dispersions, or can be dissolved in kerosene for use as a spray. Dicophane is slow in action, but exerts an effect for a long time after the spraying has been done. Gamma benzene hexachloride has a quick action, but it must be used more often, as its residual effect is short.

Trichomoniasis; is an infection of the vagina and vulva treated by **Metronidazole** 200 mg. tds for 7 days; it cures 80 per cent when given orally. Specially effective during menstruation.

Impetigo, thrush and septic spots can be treated with **gentian violet** (1 per cent solution in water).

BISMUTH, MERCURY, BARIUM and CALCIUM COMPOUNDS

By J. H. Burn

Uses of bismuth:

    (*a*) For X-ray work.

    (*b*) As adsorbent powders in the intestine.

(*a*) Since bismuth is a metal with high atomic weight, it is radio-opaque, and bismuth carbonate is given as a constituent of a meal for the X-ray examination of the intestinal tract.

(*b*) Bismuth carbonate and salicylate can be used as adsorbent powders to check diarrhoea. Bismuth carbonate is a feeble antacid.

MERCURY COMPOUNDS

Uses:

(1) As purgatives.

(2) As disinfectants.

(3) Mersalyl is a diuretic.

(1) Grey Powder (finely divided mercury and chalk) is given to babies. Calomel (mercurous chloride) is given to adults. Both these have a purgative action.

(2) Mercuric chloride and mercury biniodide are inorganic salts which are used as disinfectants. They kill bacteria but are extremely slow in action. Organic mercurial disinfectants are Metaphen (nitromersol), thiomersolate (Merthiolate) and phenyl mercuric nitrate.

Barium is a metal of high atomic weight and therefore is radio-opaque. It is used for X-ray work. Only the insoluble barium sulphate must be used for a barium meal, for if by accident barium carbonate is used, some barium is absorbed into the blood stream, and death results.

Barium salts, when absorbed, cause powerful contraction of plain muscle and constriction of blood vessels.

Calcium is given by mouth as lactate and as carbonate. It is injected intravenously as gluconate. It is needed for bone formation. Milk contains 0·1 per cent calcium.

Calcium deficiency in the blood results in tetany, in which there are muscular twitches; there may be convulsions.

A fall in blood calcium occurs when the parathyroid glands are removed. Calcium excess in the blood occurs when parathyroid extract, parathormone, is injected.

When the capillaries become unduly permeable so that urticarial rashes (in summer) or chilblains (in winter) result, the administration of calcium reduces the capillary permeability.

Calcium gluconate given intravenously improves the force of the heart if the heart is weak. It augments the action of digitalis on the heart, and augments sympathetic tone.

When blood calcium is low as it may be after an operation, sympathetic impulses are ineffective. Blood transfusion containing sodium citrate is usually responsible for the low blood calcium. Give calcium lactate by mouth.

VITAMINS

Cod liver oil. The constituents are:

(1) iodine (this is present in most fish tissues)
(2) vitamin A
(3) vitamin D.

Cod liver oil was used for its beneficial action on the respiratory tract during the nineteenth century before the discovery of vitamins. It is given to patients with chronic bronchitis, or to those prone to bronchitis or pneumonia, and has very great value in convalescence after respiratory infections. It is useful in the treatment of rickets, because of its vitamin D content.

Vitamin A is formed in the body from carotene. In adult human subjects vitamin A deficiencies are rarely observed. Some forms of night blindness are believed to be due to such a deficiency.

A group of 20 subjects was kept on a diet deficient in vitamin A for nearly two years during the war. No symptoms, however, occurred.

Vitamin D. The pure vitamin is used medicinally as *calciferol*. It is used

(1) in rickets,
(2) in lupus,
(3) in the treatment of spontaneous fractures.

Uses:

Vitamin D is given to children as a prophylactic against rickets.

In the treatment of lupus (a tubercular infection of the skin of the nose) very large amounts of vitamin D are given, in the neighbourhood of 50,000 units daily. There is a risk that the administration of these large doses will lead to calcium deposition in the kidney.

In young adults spontaneous fractures may occur, which can also be treated by giving very large doses of vitamin D. These fractures must be distinguished from those caused by a para-thyroid tumour.

Vitamin B. The different members of this group are:

> aneurine or thiamine (B_1)
> riboflavin
> inositol
> nicotinic acid
> para-aminobenzoic acid
> pantothenic acid
> pyridoxine.

Deficiency of aneurine (thiamine) leads to polyneuritis and beri-beri. (Recently large doses, 25 mg. four times daily, have been used for lumbago and similar conditions.)

Deficiency of nicotinic acid leads to pellagra.

Deficiency of riboflavin leads to corneal vascularization.

Vitamin C is ascorbic acid. It is used in the treatment of scurvy, the symptoms of which are bleeding of the gums, and painful swollen joints around which haemorrhage occurs. It is used in the treatment of benzene poisoning.

There appears to be a difference between ascorbic acid and the natural vitamin C, and this difference is believed by some to be explained by the association of vitamin P with vitamin C in natural sources of vitamin C. A lack of vitamin P is said to make the subject liable to capillary haemorrhages. This liability can be estimated by observing the effect of restricting the venous return in the arm on a patch of skin in the forearm. If the capillary walls are fragile, this restriction produces a number of capillary haemorrhages in the space of half an hour.

A tendency to capillary haemorrhages is considered important in those with a raised blood pressure, as they become more liable to cerebral haemorrhages.

Rutin is a substance which corrects this deficiency, and which may be vitamin P.

Vitamin K is necessary for the formation of prothrombin in the liver. Menaphthone (menadione) is a synthetic substance, methylnaphthoquinone, which has the same action. Aceto-menaphthone and nicotinic acid are used together in the treatment of chilblains.

CLINICAL TRIALS

THE following account is the classical example of how a clinical trial should be carried out.

A problem which arose after the introduction of streptomycin concerned its value in the treatment of tuberculosis. Was it certain that it accelerated recovery? To solve this, an investigation was arranged by the British Medical Research Council. Patients with a similar degree of pulmonary tuberculosis were selected, numbering 107 in all. They were divided into two groups, one containing 55 subjects and one containing 52 subjects. Both groups were treated alike, except that the first group received 0·5 g. streptomycin by intramuscular injection at intervals of 6 hours (i.e. four times a day) during a period of 6 months. The purpose of these injections was not explained. The second group were not injected. They were the controls, but they did not know that they were controls.

The temperature, particularly the evening temperature, is high in tuberculosis; it was observed that on the average the temperature fell more in those who were treated during the course of the 6 months. Another index of disease is the erythrocyte sedimentation rate (ESR). This also fell more in those who were treated. The number of bacteria in the sputum also declined more rapidly in those who were treated.

The main evidence obtained, however, was of a different kind. When a patient is infected with tuberculosis his lungs do not remain clear when examined by X-rays. Healthy lungs are full of air and are not seen. But as tuberculosis develops the lung becomes inflamed and thickened and this thickening is seen in a photograph taken by X-rays. The severity of the disease can therefore be judged by the amount of thickening. Consequently, X-ray photographs or radiographs of the chest of each patient were taken at the beginning of the trial. Other radiographs were taken at the end of 2 months, at the end of 4 months and at the end of 6 months. Three experts each compared the four radiographs of each patient to form an opinion whether each patient had improved. These three experts did not know whether any photograph they were examining came from a patient who was one of those who was being treated with streptomycin or whether it came from one of the controls. The results are shown in Table 1.

TABLE 1
RESULTS OF X-RAY EXAMINATION

	Treated patients	Control patients
0–2 months	76 per cent improved	6 per cent improved
0–4 months	78 per cent improved	21 per cent improved
0–6 months	69 per cent improved	33 per cent improved

Table 1 shows that a much higher percentage of patients improved who were treated with streptomycin than who were not treated. In the 6 months period there were deaths and these were divided among the two groups as shown in Table 2. The deaths were fewer among those who were treated.

TABLE 2
DEATHS IN SIX MONTHS

	Treated patients	Control patients
Number of cases	55	52
Number of deaths	4	14
Percentage of deaths	7·3	26·9

These results were a clear demonstration that streptomycin was a valuable agent in the treatment of tuberculosis. Once this was proved, further observations continued to support the evidence. To-day it is hard to realize that there was a time when there was doubt about this question. It is difficult to exaggerate the importance of knowing for certain that a drug is effective. Once that question has been settled, so that it is no longer a bone of contention, rapid strides have always been made in obtaining much better results. As an example of an agent about which similar information was never obtained, we may take sodium gold thiosulphate. This was used for many years despite uncertainty whether it was effective. However, now it has been agreed that it is useless in the treatment of tuberculosis.

SIMPLE STATISTICAL CONSIDERATIONS

The meaning of standard deviation

In making a volumetric titration, the figures obtained when the titration is repeated two or three times are not identical, but not very wide apart. Thus they may be 14·9, 15·0 and 15·2. In making biological measurements the differences are greater. The amounts of cocaine required to cause the death of different cats were found to be 42·4, 45·2, 48·4, 53·5 and 98·2 mg. per kg. when given by slow intravenous injection in the spinal animal. Similarly, the systolic blood pressure of five students examined in a class was 106, 115, 128, 135 and 145 mm.

The results for the cocaine and the results for the systolic blood pressure can be expressed by taking the mean or average result. Thus the mean figure for cocaine is 57·5 mg. per kg., and the mean figure for systolic blood pressure is 125·8. But these mean figures give no idea how scattered are the figures from which they were calculated. Thus the mean figure for blood pressure might have been the mean of figures all close together, say between 123 and 129. When a mean figure is given in a book or a report, there should always be something to indicate whether the mean is a mean of figures very close together, or whether it is a mean of figures scattered wide part. Often the indication is given as a figure after the mean, thus 25·5 ± 5·6. This figure is a measure of the scatter of the figures which give the mean. It is the standard deviation.

How to measure scatter

A simple way to obtain an idea of the scatter of the figures is to calculate how much each figure differs from the mean, and to work out the average difference. Statisticians do not speak of 'difference,' but prefer the term 'deviation', so it is possible to work out the average deviation. Thus for the cocaine figures we have

Mean	Observations	Deviation
57·5	42·4	15·1
	45·2	12·3
	48·4	9·1
	53·5	4·0
	98·2	40·7

81·2 = sum of deviations.

By adding together the deviations, we obtain 81·2 as the sum, and the average deviation is this number divided by 5, or 16·2. In statistical terminology we have calculated the average deviation by using the formula $\dfrac{Sd}{n}$; d means deviation, S means the sum of, and Sd means 'the sum of the deviations'; n is the number of observations.

We can now express the results for cocaine by saying the amount needed to kill a spinal cat by slow intravenous injection is 57·5 ± 16·2 mg. per kg. This expression gives the mean result and also the scatter of the figures.

The standard deviation

Statisticians do not, in fact, use the average deviation. To provide a measure of scatter, they use something essentially the same but slightly more elaborate. They use the standard deviation. This is standard only in the sense that it is an agreed form of expressing the deviation. Having worked out each deviation, they square it, and then find the sum of the squares of the deviations. They divide this sum by the number of observations (less one) and then take the square root. This is the standard deviation, and it is nothing more than a measure of scatter, like the average deviation. The standard deviation is

$$\sqrt{\dfrac{Sd^2}{n-1}}$$

whereas the average deviation is $\dfrac{Sd}{n}$.

The standard deviation usually makes the scatter look greater than the average deviation makes it look. Thus for the cocaine figures, using the standard deviation we have $57 \cdot 5 \pm 23 \cdot 1$ mg. per kg., instead of $57 \cdot 5 \pm 16 \cdot 2$ mg. per kg.

The standard error

We have now seen what the standard deviation is. It is a measure of the scatter of the individual figures which go to make the mean. There is another term, the standard error, which has a different object. It is intended to provide an idea of the inaccuracy of the mean. We obtained a mean figure for the amount of cocaine that is needed to kill a spinal cat, a figure, that is to say, for the lethal dose of cocaine, by observation on five cats. If we were to take five cats more we would obtain a slightly different figure. The true mean could only be obtained by making observations, say, on one thousand cats; the mean so obtained would be true in the sense that it would not be appreciably altered by taking one or two cats more. We cannot, however, take one thousand cats, and we wish to have an idea, an estimate, of the inaccuracy of the mean which we obtain from the few cats we do take.

What is meant by the inaccuracy of the mean? It is the extent to which the mean will vary if a series of experiments is done, each on a limited number of cats. Now it is clear that the inaccuracy of the mean, or the standard error of the mean as the statisticians call it, will be proportional to the scatter of the figures which make the mean. Hence the standard error of the mean will be proportional to the standard deviation. But the standard error of the mean will clearly also depend on the number of animals used. The larger the number of animals used the less the error. If each experiment is carried out on twenty cats, the mean results obtained will differ from each other less than if each experiment is carried out on only five cats. Hence we can say that the standard error of the mean is proportional to the standard deviation and inversely proportional to the number of animals used. Unfortunately the error does not diminish in direct proportion to the number of animals used,

K*

but only in proportion to the square root of the number. If a result has been obtained on four animals, the error of the mean result is not halved unless sixteen animals are taken.

If s be taken as the standard deviation, and if e be taken as the standard error

$$s = \sqrt{\frac{Sd^2}{n-1}}$$

$$\text{and } e = \frac{1}{\sqrt{n}} \times s$$

$$\text{or } e = \sqrt{\frac{Sd^2}{n(n-1)}}$$

this formula gives a numerical estimate of the extent to which the mean is likely to vary when an experiment on n animals is repeated.

The significance of a difference

It often happens that when two similar substances are compared to see which is the stronger, it is necessary to decide whether the mean results for the two substances differ by a significant amount. For example, two tinctures of strophanthus were tested by the cat method. In this method tincture is administered by slow intravenous injection to a series of anaesthetized cats, and the amount of tincture just sufficient to arrest the heart is determined. Previous to administration each tincture was diluted 900 times. The amounts of diluted tincture expressed per kg. of cat body weight were as follows:

Tincture A	Tincture B
13·9 c.c.	21·8
14·2	16·7
15·4	18·0
13·0	20·4
11·2	15·3
17·0	13·3
21·0	19·8

The mean of the figures for tincture A is 15·1 and for tincture B is 17·9. Hence more of tincture B was needed than of tincture A to have a lethal effect on the cat. Hence tincture B appears to be weaker than tincture A.

Is this really so? Is tincture A really stronger than tincture B? Is the difference between 15·1 and 17·9 a difference which is *significant*? Or is the difference due to variation in the cats used? Were the cats used for tincture A a different sample of cats from the sample of cats used for tincture B? Is the difference between 15·1 and 17·9 a difference which is due to the 'error of sampling'?

The answer to this can be seen most simply by expressing the position graphically. OA is taken to represent the lethal dose of tincture A and OB that of tincture B.

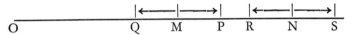

| | C | A | D | B | E |

The value OA has a standard error which is indicated by AC and AD; the value OB has a standard error indicated by BD and BE. If the value OA is redetermined, it may be found as great as OD, and if the value OB is redetermined it may be found as small as OD. Thus it is obvious that the difference between the two means, the difference between OB and OA, which is AB, is not significant, if this difference is not greater than the sum of the standard errors.

If one mean is m_1 and the other mean is m_2, then $m_1 - m_2$ must be greater than $e_1 + e_2$, or $\dfrac{m_1 - m_2}{e_1 + e_2}$ must be greater than 1.

Now consider a second picture

| | Q | M | P | R | N | S |

In this second figure OM represents one mean and ON the second. MP and MQ are the standard error of the first mean, and NS, NR of the second. The difference between the two means, which is MN, is clearly about twice as great as the sum of the standard errors, and the difference NM is significant.

To determine significance, statisticians do not use the formula

$$\frac{m_1 - m_2}{e_1 + e_2}$$

but they use the formula

$$\frac{m_1 - m_2}{\sqrt{e_1^2 + e_2^2}}$$

which is called t. When t has been calculated it is best to consult Fisher and Yates *Statistical Tables for Biological, Agricultural and Medical Research* in which a table of the 'Distribution of t' is given. As a rough rule, however, when t=2 or more, it can be concluded that the difference between the samples which has been observed would not arise by chance more often than 1 in 20 trials. That is to say, if one tincture was tested on seven cats on twenty different occasions, the results would not differ by an amount such that t would be as great as two in more than one of the trials.

Variation in response to drugs

The pharmacopoeial doses for drugs give the false impression that a given dose always produces the same effect. It is assumed that a patient who receives 0·5 mg. atropine sulphate (1/120 grain) is fully 'atropinized'. This is not so; this dose may be too little or it may be unnecessarily large, as is evident from those cases where it has been possible to test the point. Paxson (1932) determined the amount of amytal required to produce narcosis in women in labour. He injected sodium amytal (sodium *iso*-amylethyl-barbiturate) intravenously at a slow rate until a certain degree of narcosis was obtained, and calculated the amount per kg. of the patient's weight. One patient required as little as 5 mg. per kg.; another required as much as 19 mg. per kg. Others required intermediate amounts, most needing 10–12 mg. per kg. Thus one extreme was almost four times the other.

The results show in addition that even when the dose is varied according to the body weight, the differences between patients are not appreciably less.

There is a similar variation in the dose of a drug which produces toxic effects. Hanzlik (1913) has investigated the amount of sodium salicylate which produced toxic effects, such as headache, vomiting and tinnitus. Among 400 patients, some showed symptoms after 2·6 gm. (40 grains) while others required as much as 31 gm. (470 grains) before symptoms occurred; thus some were unaffected by ten times the dose which produced symptoms in others.

The use of the standard deviation

When the standard deviation is known it gives useful information. In 1923 Alvarez published tables showing the variation in systolic blood pressure of 6,000 men between the ages of 16 and 40 years in the University of California. The lowest was 85 mm. Hg and the highest was 194 mm. Hg. To exclude the possibility that the higher blood pressures were due to disease among the older men, Alvarez recorded separately the pressures in 1,215 students, all of 18 years of age, and found that the range of variation was almost the same, namely, from 85 mm. to 184 mm. The number of persons with very low blood pressures was small; the number steadily rose for blood pressures up to 120 mm. and then after 134 mm. it fell. Between 120 and 134 mm. was the most fashionable range of blood pressure, hence called by statisticians the 'mode'. To be in this range is to be 'à la mode'. When a curve was plotted relating successive ranges of blood pressure (expressed on the abscissa) to the number of persons whose blood pressure fell within that range (expressed on the ordinate), the curve was roughly bell-shaped. It was a frequency curve showing the relative frequency with which a particular blood pressure was met.

An ideal frequency curve is shown in the accompanying figure. The average systolic blood pressure found by Alvarez was 120 mm. and the standard deviation was ±13·5 mm. In the

figure the point B corresponds to the mean value 129 mm. and
BD and BC are distances equal to the standard deviation 13·5 mm.
The point D corresponds to a blood pressure of 115·5 mm. and
the point C to a blood pressure of 142·5 mm. If perpendiculars

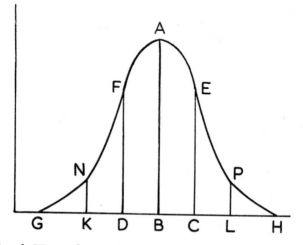

DF and CE are drawn, then the area AFDCE is found to be
approximately twice the sum of the areas FGD and ECH. This
fact means that if we examine the blood pressure of any healthy
man the value found is twice as likely to lie between 115·5 mm.
and 142·5 mm. as to be less than 115·5 mm. or greater than
142·5 mm. Or if we examine three healthy men, the blood
pressure of two of them is likely to be between 115·5 mm. and
142·5 mm., while the blood pressure of the third will be either
less than 115·5 mm. or greater than 142·5 mm. Or if we examine
six healthy men, the blood pressure of four of them is likely to
lie between 115·5 mm. and 142·5 mm., the blood pressure of the
fifth is likely to be less than 115·5 mm., and the blood pressure
of the sixth is likely to be more than 142·5 mm. Thus according
to the statistical theory one-sixth or 16 per cent of all healthy
men are likely to have a blood pressure greater than 142·5 mm.

We can compare this prophecy with the observations made by Alvarez. He found actually that 22 per cent of men had a blood pressure greater than 140 mm., which is not bad agreement between theory and fact.

Returning to the figure, KB and BL are each made equal to twice the standard deviation. If perpendiculars KN and LP are drawn, then the area ANKLP is found to be approximately 21 times the sum of the areas NGK and PLH. If we subtract twice the standard deviation (which is 27) from the mean blood pressure, we find that K corresponds to 102 mm.; similarly L corresponds to (129 + 27 =) 156 mm. Then if we examine the blood pressure of 22 healthy men, we can prophesy that the blood pressure of 21 of them will be found to lie between 102 mm. and 156 mm., while the blood pressure of the twenty-second man will be either less than 102 mm. or greater than 156 mm. Similarly if we examine the blood pressure of 44 men, the blood pressure of 42 will lie between 102 and 156 mm., while one will have a pressure less than 102 mm., and one will have a pressure greater than 156 mm. Thus, according to the statistical theory, one man in 44 will have a blood pressure greater than 156 mm. Alvarez actually found that a blood pressure greater than 160 mm. occurred in one man in 36.

Thus, if men in Britain are similar to men in the University of California, it follows that when a doctor examines applicants for life insurance, he will find that somewhere about one man in 40 will have a systolic blood pressure greater than 160 mm. It will be wrong to say that this man is suffering from hypertension, for he may have had the same blood pressure when he was in his teens. It will be most important not to suggest to the man that he is suffering from hypertension. However, it will be wise to arrange to make a second examination after some months to see if his blood pressure is rising. The diagnosis of hypertension must be made only on evidence that the blood pressure is rising. It may be asked what view the insurance company should take of the life of a man who has a systolic blood pressure of 150 mm. or 160 mm. which is not rising. It is probably true that the man is exposed to greater risks, in the same way as those unusually tall are more likely to knock their heads. But present evidence gives no clear answer to this question.

The 'Chi Squared' Test

In many tests it is impossible to give a numerical expression to the effect of treatment in each patient. For example, it may only be possible to divide the patients into those who survive and those who die. When coronary thrombosis occurs, it is usual to give the patient heparin by intravenous injection for the first day, and to administer dicoumarol or tromexan by mouth to reduce the clotting power of the blood. This treatment is troublesome because it is necessary to measure the prothrombin in the blood every day to ensure that it does not fall too low. The question then arises whether the therapy is worth while.

An investigation was therefore carried out in which 432 patients were treated and 368 were controls. Some of the patients in each group survived and some died. The figures are given in Table 3.

TABLE 3

NUMBER OF INDIVIDUALS

	Treated	Not treated	Total
Number surviving	367 (a)	280 (c)	647 (a + c)
Number died	65 (b)	88 (d)	153 (b + d)
	432 (a + b)	368 (c + d)	

In the treated group 14·9 per cent died, while in the untreated group 24 per cent died. The question then arises is this difference significant, or could it have occurred by chance? Now it is clear that if the treatment really helps, the number surviving who are treated and the number of controls dying should be respectively higher than the number of controls surviving and the number of treated dying. Taking the lettering in the table, the product ad should be greater than the product bc. Thus ad—bc should be positive and proportional to the benefit given by treatment. The following formula is applied:

$$\chi^2 = \frac{(ad - bc)^2 (a + b + c + d)}{(a + b)(a + c)(c + d)(b + d)}$$

When the result for the figures in Table 3 is calculated, χ^2 is 10·1, and when the table of χ^2 in *Statistical Tables for Biological, Agricultural and Medical Research* is consulted, P is found to be 0·0016, which means that the difference between treated and controls which was observed would not arise by chance more often than 1 in 630 such trials. Therefore the treatment is worth while.

Psychological effects

It is often found in trials where dummy tablets are used that these have a beneficial effect. For example, Jellinek described a research to discover which was the more effective of two substances A and B which were put in a tablet for the relief of headache. A trial was carried out on 199 patients using four different tablets; one tablet contained A + B; a second contained A; a third contained B and the fourth contained lactose only; it was the dummy tablet. The patients all had frequent headaches, and they were divided into four groups, each group being tested for 2 weeks on one of the tablets. After 8 weeks, all patients had tried all the tablets. The results are shown in Table 4.

TABLE 4
PERCENTAGE OF HEADACHES CURED

Tablet	199 *patients*	79 *patients*
A + B	84	**88**
A	80	77
B	86	67
Lactose	52	0

The interesting observation was therefore made that 52 per cent of headaches were cured when the dummy tablets containing lactose were taken. The other tablets had a greater effect but they were all similar to one another in efficacy. However, the patients were then sorted out into two groups, those who were benefited with the dummy tablets and those who were not. The former were excluded on the ground that observations in them were obscured by the psychological effect and could not be used to differentiate between the tablets. There were 79 patients who found no relief of headache when they took the dummy tablets. The results in them are shown in Table 4, and they indicate that the combination A + B was best, that A alone was next best, and B alone was third best. Thus by excluding patients who found relief by taking dummy tablets, an answer to the question was found.

METHODS OF ADMINISTRATION

THE concentration of a drug in the blood rises most rapidly after

    (a) intravenous,
then (b) intramuscular,
then (c) subcutaneous,
then (d) oral administration.

But the variation in the rise of the concentration in the blood differs for different substances. For example, the rise of anti-toxin (e.g. diphtheria antitoxin) in the blood after subcutaneous or intramuscular injection is very slow. Three days is required by these routes to reach the level obtained by intravenous injection at the same time. Ergometrine, on the other hand, is very rapidly absorbed into the blood no matter how it is given. Even when given by mouth it exerts an action on the uterus in 4 minutes.

METHODS OF PROLONGING THE EFFECT OF AN INJECTION

Many substances when injected have a very short action because they are excreted or destroyed. Often their effect can be prolonged by injecting them in a combination from which they are slowly released, or in a solution from which they escape into the blood slowly.

Examples:

(1) Insulin injected as protamine insulin or zinc-protamine-insulin.
(2) Diphtheria toxoid precipitated on alumina is injected as APT (alum-precipitated-toxoid).
(3) Desoxycorticosterone acetate is injected in oily solution.
(4) Desoxycorticosterone acetate is implanted as tablets under the skin.

(5) Penicillin is injected in aqueous suspension as a compound
    with procaine.
It is possible to delay the excretion of substances by the kidney.
The only example is the use of probenecid to delay the excretion
of penicillin. Probenecid saturates the capacity of the kidney
to excrete, and penicillin remains in the blood.

EQUIVALENTS, Etc.

1 gramme   is 15 grains
1 grain   is 64 milligrammes
1 c.c. (or ml.) is 15 minims

1 drachm is 4 cc. (or ml.)
1 ounce   is 30 cc. or 8 drachms
1 pint   is 600 cc. or 20 ounces
1 litre   is 1·76 pints

1 kilogramme is 2·2 pounds

1 drachm is 1 teaspoon
2 drachms is 1 dessertspoon
1 ounce   is 2 tablespoons

Physiological saline contains 0·9 per cent NaCl.
Milk contains 0·1 per cent calcium
Blood contains 0·1 per cent dextrose

1 pint milk provides 400 calories

Cow's milk contains 3 per cent protein, 4 per cent fat, 5 per cent lactose
Human milk contains 1·7 per cent protein, 4 per cent fat, 7 per cent lactose

1 per cent means 1 g. in 100 cc.
         or   1000 mg. in 100 cc.
         or   10 mg. in 1 cc.

10^{-5} means $\dfrac{1}{10^5}$

  or 1 g. in 10^5

  or 1 g. in 100,000 cc.

  or 1000 mg. in 100,000 cc.

  or 1 mg. in 100 cc.

  or 1000 micrograms in 100 cc.

  or 10 micrograms in 1 cc. (i.e. 10γ per cc.)

INDEX

INDEX